The Best of Sean Patrick

Memories of Growing Up Catholic

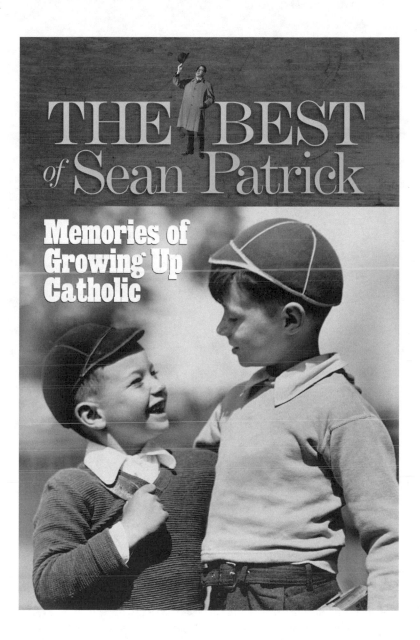

THE BEST
of Sean Patrick

Memories of Growing Up Catholic

TWENTY-THIRD PUBLICATIONS

185 WILLOW STREET • PO BOX 180 • MYSTIC, CT 06355
TEL: 1-800-321-0411 • FAX: 1-800-572-0788
 E-MAIL: ttpubs@aol.com • www.twentythirdpublications.com

282
PAT

Twenty-Third Publications
A Division of Bayard
185 Willow Street
P.O. Box 180
Mystic, CT 06355
(860) 536-2611
(800) 321-0411
www.twentythirdpublications.com

ISBN:1-58595-247-8
Library of Congress Catalog Card Number: 2002111932
Printed in the U.S.A.

Dedication

To the people of Patrick's Corner;
to my wife, Patricia;
to Kathleen and Chris, on the occasion of their marriage!
to the readers who became a part of our lives.

Acknowledgments

First off, it is absolutely necessary to say a sincere "thanks" to *Catholic Digest*, the magazine in which my series is published, and especially to Richard Reece, the editor-in-chief. In my fifteen years' association with this fine magazine I have watched it grow from super to phenomenal in quality. To Nick Cafarelli, senior associate editor; to Marge France, the former administrative assistant who smoothed the paperwork path and made life a whole lot easier.

I can't leave out my family, especially my wife, Trish, who put up with the idiosyncrasies of a writer and who encouraged me at every single step. She is really the power behind the throne (whatever that means).

And mostly, to the readers of *Catholic Digest* who wrote to me, who let me know when I was on target and when I was a bit out in left field. Really, this book is for you.

Contents

Part II: The Parish Family of St. Columbkille

Foreword

Patrick's Corner is a chunk of sidewalk in Cleveland, Ohio, where busy crosstown streetcars and buses whiz by throughout the day, carrying their passengers to the far-flung parts of our great city. Here the six Patrick brothers shined shoes and hawked newspapers, passing the torch down from the eldest boy, Tommy, to Billy and then to David, then to Kevin and on to Danny, who eventually gave it to me, the youngest in the family.

We grew and thrived on Patrick's Corner among people who were like us and others who were quite different. Here we mixed and lived, rejoiced and grieved, worked, played, and worshiped in the only world we knew. Life was hard sometimes, but never so hard that we could not cope.

As time passed, we became solid in our ways, strong in our faith, and dedicated to each other and the world we loved—the world of Patrick's Corner. Bloke, my best friend and constant companion during those growing-up years, put it well when he said, "Friendship is like the sands of time, Sean-o. It's always moving but it's always there."

Come in, now, and meet Bloke and Mama and my brothers. Enjoy the friendship of Ritchie and Noam Saperstein, "Din" (Denis) Tracy, who was the son of the local Presbyterian minister. Laugh at the always humble and always lovable Father Francis X. O'Phelan, who made holiness seem like a common piece of the fabric of life. Meet his boss, Monsignor Hanratty, made of the stuff a leader needed, a pillar upon which many of us leaned in times of sorrow or of trial. And I can't forget Charlie, Victor, Regan—who shared my life and whom I am still proud to know and love.

So, welcome to Patrick's Corner. You are part of my world now.

Cast of Characters

The Patricks

Sean Patrick, the author

Tommy Patrick, eldest brother, served in the Navy in Korea

Billy Patrick

David Patrick

Kevin Patrick

Daniel Patrick, next to Sean in age, best friend

Mama Patrick

St. Columbkille's Parish

Father Guilhooley, founding pastor

Edward Guilhooley, his Irish setter

Monsignor Hanratty, pastor

Father Francis X. O'Phelan, senior assistant pastor

Kevin O'Phelan, Father O'Phelan's dog, named for Kevin Patrick

Sister St. Patrick, eighth-grade teacher, in charge of altar boys

Sister St. Chantal, teacher

Sister St. Gabriel, seventh-grade teacher

Sister St. Enda, second-grade teacher

Sister St. Kermit, principal

Finneran, custodian

Neighborhood Friends

Bloke Callahan, Sean's best friend

Charlie Carroll

Regan O'Farrell

Victor Doyle, a British war orphan

Duffy (Dorian Fitzhugh), friend of Kevin's, like another brother

Brian O'Neill

Ritchie and Noam Saperstein

Denis "Din" Tracy

Jim Hoch

Joey and Steven Stolarski

Other Residents of Patrick's Corner

John-the-Hardware, owner of the hardware store

Mr. Munstein, owner of the grocery store

Mr. Ott, butcher

Father Joseph, a Franciscan, runs downtown mission

Brother Dismas, another Franciscan

Mr. Stolarski, Joey and Steven's father, who is in a wheelchair

Mr. Mulrennan, older parishioner, becomes altar server

Mrs. O'Malley, downstairs neighbor of the Patricks

Reverend Martin Tracy, Presbytarian minister

Rabbi Hirsch

Reverend Hoch, Lutheran minister

Introduction

After almost forty years away, I found that the old neighborhood still held some nostalgic remnants for me. I had returned for the funeral of Mr. Carroll, Charlie's father, who was being laid to rest from my old parish of St. Columbkille, even though the family had not lived in the area for three decades or more.

I had visited the funeral home the evening before and had had a chance to visit with Charlie, who had become a priest in a missionary order. He was home from the missions, however, and teaching in the seminary of his order in Washington, D.C. Like the rest of us, he looked a bit older. Gray strands flecked his still-fiery red hair. The boyhood freckles were less prominent but Charlie was still Charlie and I kept waiting for him to trip on the cassock he was wearing.

My brothers and their families came, one by one, until we were all there. Bloke, my best friend, sidled up next to me and poked me in the ribs. He had a couple of his grandchildren he and his wife were "baby-sitting" with them. I could not help but see how little had changed and how much of the Callahans was passed on in the twin nine-year-olds wearing their uncomfortable neckties.

Brian O'Neill was there with his wife. I remembered how we had gathered for the funeral of his little brother, Regis, and how the crowds of kids had stood weeping regardless of faith or background. Brian was one of us, and his loss was ours.

Din—the Reverend Denis Tracy, who was my brother Danny's best friend—came to the wake with his wife. He was still pastor of the Hardin Street Presbyterian Church, which his father had founded. He was the only one of us who had stayed in the old neighborhood, and he served God's people just as his father had. And like his father, he was a model of holiness and Christlike living.

I felt myself being swept up in a bear hug and I looked into the gleaming eyes of Ritchie Saperstein, one of my oldest friends. I had not seen him for a few years. Tears flowed freely as we embraced and told each other how glad we were to be there together. Noam, Ritchie's younger brother who was now an Orthodox Rabbi, had come in from Toledo for the funeral—and an excuse to see his old friends.

As the evening wore on, more and more friends from our old neighborhood came in, and as more and more words were spoken we found ourselves whisked back into the world of our growing-up days. Our neighborhood was a place where wealth was counted in pennies, nickels, and dimes, seldom in dollars and never in stocks, bonds, or certificates of deposit. Sharing was expected and was a way of life. Those who had shared with those who did not: it was as simple as that.

There were a lot of kids at the funeral home that night. Some of them were our grandchildren but others were the grandchildren of people we did not know. Still, the children all mingled and laughed together, taking over the wide porch of the funeral home to talk and play games while us "old folks" stayed inside to catch up with one another's lives.

It did not dawn on me until much later that it seemed as if only a little time had passed since I was young. Now here I was, among the patriarchs, the parents, the "auld" people.

Others were there whom we did not know, people "up" from Mingo County, West Virginia, the old homeland of the Carrolls. At first they stood uneasily, somewhat self-consciously, until Charlie introduced them and they became one of us. Their accents marked them as "mountain folk," but their shining eyes marked them as kin to us all.

At the funeral Mass the next day, I was gratified to see just how little St. Columbkille had changed. There was an altar in the front of the sanctuary, of course, but the ornate marble altar we knew so well was still in its place at the back of the sanctuary.

Charlie was the celebrant for his father's funeral Mass. I shook my head and grinned when I heard Charlie mention that his dad had been eighty-eight years old. His mother, still beautiful—in fact more so, as her age enhanced her gentle and patient bearing—sat half-smiling, remembering the years she and her husband had shared.

At the cemetery we crowded together and prayed as we watched my brother Tommy's grandson, Brendan, perform the Walk of the Piper, a tradition at an Irish funeral. The fifteen-year-old walked the stiff, gaited step-dip-march as had his own great-uncle David when he, too, was fifteen, at a burial in this very cemetery.

Seeing everyone at the funeral gave me pause to think about the people I had known and loved while growing up. We were a mixed bunch, and within this group there was little room for bigotry or haughtiness.

And yet I had known bigotry. I had seen the swastikas painted on the Temple less than a block from St. Columbkille. I had heard a bunch of kids taunting "Christ killers" as they passed the boys from the Yeshiva.

I pictured my Jewish friends, Ritchie and Noam. I remembered Grandfather Saperstein as he held our hands in his and made us tell him how we were doing in school, and how he listened to our troubles when we had no one else to complain to. I remembered standing with a group of altar servers around the Saperstein table celebrating Passover, listening to Noam read the age old question: "Father, why is this night different from all other nights?"

I thought of the big game that our basketball team played for the city CYO championship when I was in eighth grade. We played a predominately Polish school and, for the first time in my life, I shook hands with Olsavskis, Evanowskis, Wierzchowskis, and other kids with a thousand consonants in their names! They, in turn, met the largest contingent of boys whose names began with "O" that they had ever seen. After the game, we cheered and celebrated, dowsing each other with soapy water and glorying in the fact that we had played hard, played fair, and played well.

I thought about Mama's friend, Mary, who was black. Like Mama, she washed clothes to support her family. I recalled how Mary, captured by the sudden blizzard of 1949, stayed at our apartment for the night and how she taught us to sing "Blessed Assurance" in the face of adversity. Mary had two sons who were our age. Often in the summer they rode the bus with her and spent the day playing basketball or baseball with us. They were part of our lives for as long as I can remember.

We often heard disparaging remarks about the English from our sometimes excitable Irish neighbors. But then I would think of Victor Doyle, the English war orphan who entered my life when we were both in fifth grade. His nationality was unimportant to those of us who relished his genuine, glowing personality and sense of loyalty to his friends. My own life would later be bound with his when we worked as partners on the police force, depending on each other to protect our very lives.

As for the Orangemen, those dark and brooding Irishmen who were followers of King William III (that seventeenth-century upstart who tried to make Ireland a Protestant country) and who were supposedly anathema to "our" kind, I only had to think of Denis ("Din") Tracy and his family. His father, the Reverend Martin Tracy, exhibited all that was good, wholesome, and holy.

And now we were at the funeral of an Appalachian coal miner turned steel worker, his son one of my oldest and closest friends.

"I guess we had a pretty strange upbringing!" I said to Bloke as we stood drinking coffee at the luncheon after the burial. He knew exactly what I was talking about. Danny and Din stood nearby, laughing and talking about their lifelong friendship while their wives enjoyed each other's company.

I looked out over the crowd gathered here in the social hall of St. Columbkille. Some of the women of the parish had prepared the lavish luncheon, and I was very happy to see St. Columbkille in such good hands.

A sudden feeling of comfort flowed over me. Bloke felt it as well. "The family's growin', Sean-o!" he said softly.

I knew exactly what he meant.

Part I

The Neighborhood

The Victory Garden

For those of us who lived through World War II, the words "victo-ry garden" hold a special meaning. This term, along with catch-phrases such as "Kilroy was here" and "loose lips sink ships" repre-sent the turmoil and uncertainty that boiled around us back then.

During the war years, there was a shortage of just about every-thing. Gasoline was strictly limited and those who had automo-biles were forced to park them for all but essential travel. Each member of the family had his or her own O.P.A. ration book, which held tiny stamps that were torn out by the grocer when a purchase was made. This system ensured that each family received their fair share of rationed food, and that there would be some left for those who had not yet shopped.

Most of this didn't bother us Patrick boys because we used very few of these things in our daily lives. No one drank coffee in our house, so we gave some of our coffee stamps to friends who did. Meat was a rare treat anyway, so what we were allowed to buy was really quite generous as far as we were concerned. In all, people took care of each other and tried in various ways to help in the war effort.

We Patrick boys went from door to door collecting tin cans, which we delighted in flattening with a practiced stomp of our foot, then put the flattened cans in our wagons and carted them to a collection point. From there, we presumed they went somewhere to have something done to them so they could emerge as a shiny airplane or a battleship ready to take on the fiercest foe. Our mothers saved snippets of soap and cans of grease from cooking. This, too, was collected and used in some manner.

In the meantime, we were all encouraged to emulate our pioneer ancestors (although our own ancestors were not pioneers; they were fishermen from the Aran Isles), and try to fend for ourselves a little more. We were told that we were "soft," that we had grown used to the idea that food only came in boxes, bags, or cans found in the local grocery store. And so Americans were encouraged to return to the soil and to grow what food they could to supplement the meager rations we were permitted to buy. This was a challenge and yours truly took it seriously enough to do something about it in spite of the harshest and most gargantuan of odds.

"Where are you going to farm, Sean-o?" Danny quipped as I laid out my plan for a victory garden. "You need a barn and silo thing and horses and cows."

Even though I was not quite ten years old, I knew better than that. I explained that I did not plan to "farm" on the scale he implied. Since land was strictly limited in our tenement neighborhood, I had decided to use a plot of soil in back of our apartment building. This patch of grassless dirt was about the size of a one-car garage, and it lay next to the actual garages that were slowly decaying behind the building.

"It's sunny there and no one uses it for anything," I explained to Danny. "I asked Mr. Weber if I could use it to grow stuff." (Mr. Weber was the landlord.) Not only had Mr. Weber agreed to my plan, he also told me I could use the hose which he kept in the basement. That would make my job much easier.

I set to work with a vengeance. Using a shovel normally used for stoking the old coal furnace, I bent my back to the task of preparing the unpromising soil for the upcoming season. I dug and chopped, chopped and dug, turned and turned some more until the unforgiving, claylike dirt had been churned into a somewhat workable plot of land. I didn't know much about farming, but I had planted a bean in a paper cup in school as a science project. I knew that if you planted a seed, watered it, and let it have some sun, it would do whatever seeds do under ground to bring forth something good to eat.

Danny and Kevin had a wealth of suggestions. Danny was all set for bushels of corn on the cob, while Kevin had the unique suggestion of planting milk bottles in order to grow cows (!).

John-the-Hardware was the logical source for seeds. His hardware store was packed wall-to-wall, floor-to-ceiling with just about anything a human could want to buy. Nails, screws, chains, rope, knives, scissors, hammers, and—just up by the front door with the pleasant bell on it—a rack with packets of seeds.

One side of the rack held flower seeds. Millions of multicolored flowers seemed to jump right off the packets in a rainbow display of grandeur. But it was the other side of the rack that I was interested in. Here were envelopes with seeds for cabbages, beans, peas, lettuce, kale (whatever that is!), endive, and lots of other vegetables that looked mouthwateringly good. The lush red tomato seeds were especially tempting but there were so many varieties I had no idea where to start.

Faced with so many choices, I decided that the logical thing to do was ask John-the-Hardware, who knew everything about every item in his vast array of goods, what I should plant. No matter what my own farming intentions were, I vowed to listen to him.

"Here," John said, handing me a packet of seeds. It showed a picture of a brilliant red radish. "Radishes are an early crop and can grow pretty much through the whole season. You plant them thick and then thin them out as they grow. You stand a good chance of having a nice garden if you plant these according to the instructions on the package."

When I got back home, I opened the envelope and saw what had to be at least a million seeds. I decided to plant several packets in my victory garden so I could take advantage of every inch of soil Mr. Weber had allowed me to use.

I started out by making little lines in the soil, then put seeds in the trough formed by the lines. Then I gently covered them up and turned on the hose to water the seeds, setting the nozzle on a fine spray so the water would fall like rain instead of washing the seeds out of the ground.

Over the next few weeks, word of my radish farm spread through St. Columbkille school. Although my entire class had done the bean experiment the year before, none of us had had any real farming experience, so I was a novelty among my peers.

"Why only radishes, Mr. Patrick?" Sister St. Enda, who was the second-grade teacher, asked. "I would think you would want a grand variety of things." I explained that I was trying out my skill as a farmer and that perhaps, if I was any good at it, I might expand as the weather allowed.

To my delight, the radishes flourished. Soon the barren, dark soil was striped with lines of green shoots. As the radishes continued to grow, the green began to spread and to turn leafy.

When John-the-Hardware heard of my initial success, he came to see the garden for himself. He showed me how to thin the crop by plucking the obviously weak stems in order to make room for the stronger plants. Although I hated losing any of my precious little stems, I did as he suggested and was rewarded in a few days by thicker, stronger leaves and no significant lessening of the lines of green foliage I prized so much.

My morning and evening watering sessions had become an event as friends and family gathered to watch. Even Danny and Kevin were impressed.

"What do I do when I pick them?" I asked John one day. By now the tops of the radishes had broken through the ground and it was obviously time to begin harvesting some of them. John laughed and said, "Plant more!"

And so that evening I began pulling out the strongest and largest radishes I could find. In a short while I had filled a peck basket, and the garden looked every bit as full as before I started harvesting!

When the radishes were washed, I gave Mama the first one to try. We all watched as she carefully examined the flawless red skin of the pungent creation. Then, biting into the radish, we heard a crisp "snap." That meant my radish was firm and true. Mama smiled and I grinned back.

"It's very good, Sean!"—the ultimate compliment!

From that point on, I pulled radishes on a daily basis. Then I would smooth the soil and plant new seeds, because John had assured me that my crops would continue until the frost returned in the fall. But I soon had more radishes than I had ever seen in my life. Worse, I had no idea what to do with them.

My problem was solved and my reputation as a farmer made firm when I stopped by Mr. Munstein's grocery one day to show him a sample of my radishes. The grocer held it in his fingers and examined it for any possible flaw. He sniffed it and fluffed through the green leafy top. Then, as a final test, he carried it over to the box where other radishes lay, ready for sale.

Mr Munstein asked how many radishes I could provide, and I told him what I felt I could produce on a weekly basis. Danny, who had accompanied me on this journey, stood astounded as I made a deal with the grocer to trade my radishes for other vegetables every week.

"This way," I explained to Mama and my brothers that evening at the supper table, "my garden will give us all sorts of good things. I may only grow radishes but we end up with lettuce and celery and good stuff like that, too!"

Naturally, we kept some radishes for ourselves and gave some to our neighbors, as well as the priests and nuns at St. Columbkille. The radish supply seemed to be endless until the frost of September brought a close to my first year of "farming."

Sister St. Mary, my teacher when I returned to school in the fall, told the story of my victory garden to the entire class as I basked in the light of fame. She went on to tell how I turned my sole crop into an abundance of fresh vegetables by trading with the grocer.

I was proud of my accomplishments, but that pride was quickly tempered when Sister went on say, "So, Mr. Patrick, you were in partnership with God in a way, were you not?" I nodded and smiled.

I still have a garden. Since the time of that first "farming" experience, I feel there is something special what I have had a hand in growing.

Oh yes—even though my crops have branched out over the years, there is always space for a few radishes every time I plant.

The Hucksters

"Time for the Catholic newspaper drive," Kevin remarked one morning, noting the beginning of an annual ritual for all the schoolchildren in our diocese.

Our diocesan paper was published once a week and featured news about what was happening in the various parishes, the CYO athletic news, and the weekly Legion of Decency movie ratings (so we would know which movies we could go to see and which ones meant instant expulsion from our church if we happened to go see them anyway). The newspaper was sold by subscription only, and these sales belonged strictly to the schoolchildren of the diocese. And so for two solid weeks, just prior to Easter, we would traipse from door to door with a sample paper in hand and a pocketful of subscription blanks.

Kick off day was on a Friday. This was so the entire weekend could be devoted to blazing new trails through inspired salesmanship. Prizes were awarded to the classes in every school that sold the most subscriptions. Larger prizes, like basketballs or even a schoolwide ice cream party, were awarded to the schools who did the best job in each division.

When I was an eighth grader, St. Columbkille was seeking its third straight victory in the elementary school division, and Sister St. Patrick, our teacher, meant to see that we got it. The drive was sparked by an assembly. The entire student body was packed, pushed, and squeezed into the large gymnasium where a makeshift platform had been set up. Finneran stood by the door watching and praying that his skill in erecting the wooden platform matched the stress of teacher after teacher climbing up on the platform and challenging her class to outdo the class of the previous year.

We listened to speeches which ranged from a simple pep talk to the little tykes in the first grade, to the Knute-Rocknean "get one for the Gipper" thunder of our own Sister St. Patrick.

Sister St. Kermit, the principal, always waited until last to speak. By the time she stepped up on the platform to take the microphone from Sister St. Patrick's hand, the thousand or so students had been whipped into a frenzy and were almost begging for the subscription blanks to be handed out so they could go forth and conquer the literate world for St. Columbkille and for God.

I had heard the same speech for seven years, and my eighth-grade year was no exception. Sister St. Kermit spoke softly—we had to strain to hear her—and told us the breathtaking story of the legendary Eileen O'Grady who, singlehandedly and without infringing on any other school's protected territory, marched out of this very gym on Friday and returned on Monday morning with more than one hundred subscriptions!

Monsignor Hanratty, Father O'Phelan, and Father O'Toole always stood by the gym door during our assembly. Just before the sample copies of the newspaper were handed out with a half-dozen subscription blanks for each student, Monsignor would make his way to the platform and utter a long invocation, asking God to further "the Lord's work by inspiring these young warriors for Christ and his most Blessed Mother" to the heights of dedication and the calling of duty.

Father O'Phelan stood with his arms folded across his chest and a smug smile on his face as he watched us take our blanks and papers and head for the door, spurred on by a fifteen-minutes-early dismissal.

"So, Sean-o! Going to beat Danny's record for eighth grade, are you?" he grinned as I passed him.

"Gonna try, Father!"

I waved the thick packet of subscription blanks I had gotten from Sister St. Kermit. She knew that the Patricks had always been successful at selling subscriptions, so after a brief moment of hesitation she handed me a batch of blanks as thick as a deck of playing cards instead of the customary half-dozen allotted the mortal students.

Last year Danny sold thirty-three subscriptions during the very first weekend. Another ten sold over the next few days rounded out his endeavor and, even though he said he was going for fifty, he sloughed off a bit and ended up with forty-three in all—the eighth-grade record for that year.

We Patricks had a game plan which was a carefully guarded secret ever since Tommy, the oldest, had begun selling subscriptions on Patrick's Corner. Tommy had tried going door-to-door for a while but said that it was embarrassing to knock on someone's door only to learn that he was the fifth or sixth St. Columbkillian to bother the good people. Besides, he reasoned, it was too easy for someone to ease the door shut with a polite smile if the door was their own and the place was their castle. So, being somewhat inventive and certainly observant, he decided that it would be easier and more productive to do our selling on our own turf and at our own pace, without the threat of competition or denial.

Patrick's Corner was situated at a busy crosstown bus and streetcar exchange, a major intersection populated by a dozen or more local businesses. Back when he was just a nipper of ten, Tommy had firmly established this corner as Patrick territory, and my brothers and I had held firm on the spot, selling newspapers and shining shoes in front of the Shamrock Pub for almost a decade by the time I was in eighth grade.

Common courtesy and unspoken consent marked this spot as

exclusively Patrick. The Skully brothers, doing business just a block away, would no sooner invade Patrick's Corner than we would think of moving our shine box over to their bus stop. The Mannings had their own territory too, over by the grocery store.

And while each territory had its good and bad points, Patrick's Corner was the only territory with a pub. This was where Tommy felt we had an edge. He firmly believed that if an Irishman was an easy mark for a subscription to a Catholic newspaper, an Irishman mellowed by a couple of nips of Jamison's or Old Bushmill was an even easier mark. So he concentrated a good part of his salesmanship on the Shamrock, moving from patron to patron with a gleam in his eye and a bit of the blarney on his young lips as the railroaders nodded and handed him the two dollars for the subscription.

As the years moved on, the patrons of every business on Patrick's Corner were successfully solicited for newspaper subscriptions—Munstein's Market, Ott's Butcher Shop, John-the-Hardware—but the Shamrock was the place we counted on to make our mark.

By the time it was my turn on the Corner, the routine was so well established that I had very little to do to be a roaring success. The Shamrock was always crowded on Friday evenings. Burly railroaders, yardmen, and switchmen all crowded at the long oak bar to discuss the week and to cash their paychecks. Plumbers, firemen, and off-duty policemen mingled with their own while whole families populated the booths that lined the one wall.

When I had finished selling my papers at the bus stop, I knew there would still be a good hour of convivial socializing at the Shamrock—usually more than sufficient time for my purposes—before the place would empty out and the patrons go on to their homes for the beginning of a long-awaited weekend. Pat, the publican, saw me come in and smiled when I waved my copy of the diocesan newspaper in the air; he knew exactly why I was there.

With precision born of good example and a lot of practice, I moved slowly along the bar, displaying my sample paper with the sports news showing. In this particular issue, the sports page featured a picture of my brother Kevin during the CYO boxing tournament. Kev's athletic prowess was well known by the patrons of the Shamrock, who took great pride in calling him the "young John L. Sullivan of St. Columbkille."

"Going to take the paper, Mr. Murphy?" I would ask innocently as I pushed a subscription blank onto the bar in front of him.

From behind the bar, Pat would produce a couple of pencils and set one down by Murphy, so the poor gentleman had no real choice but to nod and write his name.

As I moved on, relentless and undaunted by the chatter of the place, the men at the bar began to put their two dollars out on the bar, and they would reach for a blank before I even got to them.

After making my rounds of the bar, I moved from booth to booth repeating my canned sales pitch, which was, for the most part, unnecessary and unheard.

People began clearing out about the time I had finished. I would repeat my visit the next day, Saturday, when a whole different crowd was there. But I didn't mind the work.

Pat brought me a grape soda while I sat on the wide windowsill sorting my subscription blanks and counting the money. My handkerchief was already spread out on the sill, waiting for the subscription money that I had to keep separate from my ordinary newspaper nickels.

"Good crowd, Sean-o," Pat said with a conspirator's grin. "How did we do today?"

"Fifty-six!" I gasped in utter amazement. It was the first time *any* Patrick had sold so many subscriptions on the first day.

Saturday produced a batch of about thirty subscriptions—but not the forty-four I had hoped for, trying to match the record of Eileen O'Grady, bless her heart.

"My goodness, Mr. Patrick!" Sister St. Patrick smiled when I dumped the contents of my handkerchief on her desk on Monday morning. "I'm surprised you still have leather on your shoes! You must have walked a hundred miles selling subscriptions this weekend!" I stood with my head bowed modestly, feeling the knowing glares of Leonard Skully and Dickie Manning who knew exactly how far I had walked.

"You others should take an example from Mr. Patrick!" she told the rest of the class. "He seems to have gone just about everywhere to spread God's holy word."

She leafed through the blanks, noting that—as usual—the addresses were not confined to my own street or neighborhood like most of my friends. To their credit, none of my classmates ever gave away our secret. I weathered their stares, their glares, and their sometimes less-than-friendly comments.

We had our ice cream party again that year: three years in a row! And I was almost sorry that my career in subscription sales was reaching a end. But I felt I could now retire, confident that I had done my part in spreading the gospel, the CYO news, and the Legion of Decency ratings along with the best of them.

The One-Hour Laundry

My dad died an untimely death on the railroad where he worked when I was a year old. This left Mama, an immigrant from the blustery Aran Isles, to raise us in the only way she knew how—as a washerwoman.

Mama was ordinarily a calm person who took things in her stride. In fact, I can't recall many occasions or circumstances that put Mama "on her ear." Nor was Mama a person who would stand in the way of progress, even though she looked on many "newfangled" things as just so much foolishness instead of as marks of the brave new world in which we lived. Many innovations were taken in stride and passed off with a quick "hmmmmmm" or "that's nice…" and promptly ignored.

Mama regarded the telephone as a novelty until we actually got one. We were almost the last family on the entire planet to have our own phone and it took begging, pleading, and ingenious arguments from all of us brothers to get it. When it arrived and we began using it, even Mama caught on to the convenience and it soon became a part of our lives, almost as if we had never been without one.

21

Mama was a laundress of some repute. She also cleaned houses, but laundry was her main calling and she went at it as any professional would his or her vocation. She took pride in her work and never seemed to complain about the hardships that made up a good part of the job.

Our place always seemed to smell of fresh-washed clothing and of the peculiar odor of ironing. The ironing board was as much a part of our furniture as the one stuffed chair and the old couch with one leg shorter than the others. Wicker baskets of clothing were set in rows; Mama always seemed to know which pile belonged to whom and which clothes needed special care.

For as long as I could remember, one or two of us were responsible for picking up or delivering laundry. We loaded the baskets in our old wagon and put fresh, clean paper over the load before hurrying down the block to the homes of the people who used Mama's service. Sometimes we were even entrusted to take the coins back to Mama, but usually the people saw her and paid her directly.

Laundry was no haphazard thing. It consisted of soaking the clothing in big tubs in our basement, boiling shirts in the copper wash boiler, mixing soaps and bleaches with an alchemist's know-how, pushing and lifting the heavy, wet garments with the bleached sticks that were a lot older than any of us.

Drying the wash was even more work. Lines were strategically run all over the backyard, taking advantage of every possible inch of space, and long poles kept the lines from sagging. Mama traveled from one end of the lines to the other with clothespins in her mouth and in her fingers as she deftly hung the clothes in the breezy air to dry stiff and sweet. In the winter, our large basement served the same purpose as the backyard, but the clothes never really came out as well as they did in "God's fresh air," which Mama felt was her personal property on the days she did wash.

All of this was suddenly threatened one spring day when the One-Hour Laundry opened up over by the Appliances by Westinghouse store near Patrick's Corner.

The place had been a beverage store that went out of business, and it had stood vacant for quite a while. Other tenants on the block were well established and so gave little thought to the vacant store. Chris' Barber Shop, the Shamrock Pub, Ott's Meats, and several other businesses had been in their locations since God had invented neighborhoods, so we all took for granted that whatever business eventually opened in the old beverage store would be something as threatening as a piece of banana cream pie. But this was not the case.

We learned of the invasion into the world of professional laundry one afternoon when we hurried into our flat to change into our work clothes before heading out to Patrick's Corner. Danny and I clopped through the open door, then stopped and stood in surprise as we saw Mrs. O'Malley, Mrs. Callahan (Bloke's mom), Mrs. O'Leary, Mrs. Feldman, and Mrs. O'Neill gathered around our table, drinking tea and commiserating with Mama, who seemed to be the chairperson of this "meeting."

"Honestly, Mrs. Patrick," one of the ladies was saying, "it just isn't right to step in and try to put you and the other ladies out of business!"

We would have stood there longer but the sudden fire in Mama's eyes when she saw us told us we had best mind our own Ps and Qs and get on with our own business.

"It's that new laundry that's going in down where the beverage store was," Kevin told us confidentially that evening. "The people can take their wash in and do it themselves in those modern washers with the glass doors and then dry it in the heated tumblers." Maybe there was trouble afoot for the local laundry ladies after all.

The new laundromat was a miracle of modern technology. There were two rows of modern washing machines with round, glass doors and a clocklike control on the top. There was a coin slot, and it cost ten cents to get the thing in motion. There wasn't a wringer in the place.

In addition to the eight or ten washers, there were four gigantic round things for drying clothes. A funny looking thing called an extractor was used to spin the clothes and take out the excess water before you put them in the dryer. Not only that, but the lady behind the counter would sell you small packets of soap powder or a cup of bleach—you didn't even have to bring your own!

"One hour, my foot!" Mama harrumphed when she stood at the window of the new place with Mrs. Callahan just before the grand opening. "It takes a good *day* to do a wash right. And what about drying? Who wants that gas smell on their fresh sheets? And I haven't seen any tubs for boiling the shirts...."

"Penny for your thoughts, ladies!"

The voice belonged to Father O'Phelan who was on his way to the Shamrock Pub to watch Bishop Fulton J. Sheen's weekly television show, *Life Is Worth Living*.

Mama snapped back to reality and told Father her thoughts on modern technology invading the sacred precincts of laundry. Mrs. Callahan added that Mama had visions of her customers hustling off to the laundromat each week with their clothes in hand instead of piling them into the baskets and waiting for us boys to pick it up.

Father stood looking in the window, watching the new owners hurrying around making sure things would be ready for their grand opening that Wednesday evening. The place was spic and span, and there were posters and signs all over the place telling one how to use the modern equipment.

Finally, their presence must have gotten the best of the new owners because one of them came to the door and asked if they—the ladies and the priest—would like to see what the place would be capable of doing. Instead of huffing that she wasn't in the least interested, Mama went into the brightly lighted place with Mrs. Callahan and Father O'Phelan. There they were introduced to the laundry of the future by the glib young man who was convinced he was placed on this earth to make life easier for humanity when it came to clean clothes.

"Why the little scales?" Father asked innocently.

The man explained that the washers could only handle so much at one time, and so the customers would have to weigh their laundry and put it in the machine one load at a time until it was all done. Father winked at Mama and she relaxed a little and went on with the tour.

Posted next to the four dryers was a list of what could and could not be put in the gas-heated tumblers.

"Seems to me they might need some clotheslines after all," Mrs. Callahan whispered to Mama.

"You might be interested in coming to the grand opening on Wednesday!" the laundromat manager told his guests. "The radio people will be here broadcasting for the whole evening. This is a very important event!"

Mama, Mrs. Callahan, and Father O'Phelan left the store and walked down the block, talking about what they had seen. "Being replaced by a machine with coins," Mama mumbled, still obviously worried about the impact of the modern world on her domain.

"Mrs. Patrick," Father O'Phelan said kindly, "do you think that these inventions will replace you? Why, I ate in an Automat restaurant a while back, a little place where the food was behind little doors and you just dropped a coin in the slot and took out whatever you wanted. No waiting, no guessing, just look and take!"

Mama and Mrs. Callahan looked puzzled.

"I was told that was where the world of dining was heading."

"Was it good, Father?" Mrs. Callahan asked.

Father laughed out loud.

"It was good, but not what I would call a fine meal. Why, I would rather sit in the Colonial Kitchen and wait for my bit of chicken and a wonderful bowl of freshly made soup!"

The ladies smiled a bit at this.

"And do you think I am worried that someday a person will be able to put a coin in a mechanical priest for Holy Communion or for confession?"

Now they actually laughed.

"People will still want the quality and personal touch. Just as they will with their priest or rabbi!"

"Still," Mama said, "a few prayers for our welfare might help, Father!"

He smiled and promised to pray for their business concerns and disappeared into the Shamrock Pub, where Bishop Sheen's program was just beginning.

On Wednesday evening Mama and Mrs. Callahan, along with several other ladies, decided that the competition needed to be taken seriously. Together, they marched up to Patrick's Corner to see what was happening. Naturally, Bloke, Danny, Kevin, Regan, Brian, Ritchie, Noam, and I had to stick our noses in the place too.

There was a good crowd of ladies and even some men in the tiny business. A local radio station had a little desk set up and, between songs played from some location far from the laundromat, a famous gentleman would talk to the people and ask them what they thought about the modern world coming at last to our neighborhood Mama and her cohorts wisely stayed a good distance from the broadcasting desk.

Mr. Ellis, the manager, explained several times how the place worked, how you put your clothes in measured amounts into one of the boxlike machines, how you added soap and then put the coin in the slot. Then, after the machine was finished, how you "extracted" great amounts of water in the extractor (for only a dime) and then put them in one of the four massive drying machines where they would tumble in gas warmth until they were fluffy and dry.

A lady who was obviously part of the store was demonstrating on one machine while Mrs. Lenehan, always one to test out new and interesting things, was busy washing her kitchen rugs. The professional laundry lady continued her demonstration and Mrs. Lenehan went about her business. We all watched as she lifted the heavy rugs out of the washer and carried them, dripping, to the extractor and dropped a dime into the slot. The machine whirred and vibrated as the rugs were spun so fast that water was sucked out, leaving the rugs half as heavy as they had been coming out of the machine.

"Can your machine dry these?" Mrs. Lenehan asked the distracted manager who assured her that they would be dry as dust in a very short time.

We continued watching the laundry lady's demonstration while Mrs. Lenehan busied herself loading her kitchen rugs into a large dryer. She then set the thing in motion simply by dropping a coin in the slot.

The demonstration was just about finished and we were just about bored enough to go out into the cool evening air when the first wisps of smoke reached someone's nostrils.

"FIRE!" a lady in a gingham housedress hollered.

Sure enough, smoke was rapidly filling the little laundromat. The smoke was belching from the dryer tumbling around Mrs. Lenehan's kitchen rugs, and the white, metal sides of the dryer had suddenly turned an ominous brown.

Mr. Ellis leaped at the big door and yanked it open. Flames burst out and the ladies started a swift evacuation from the store, almost trampling the famous gentleman from the radio station who was telling his listeners about the incredible scene taking place right before his very eyes.

We later learned that Mrs. Lenehan had rubber-backed rugs in her kitchen, which was something that the sign had neglected to warn against putting in the dryer.

When the excitement was over and the radio gentleman had packed his things and left for his station, the laundromat was left quite empty. Mr. Ellis and the demonstration lady were busy sweeping up rug debris from the floor, and the fire department put a big fan in the doorway to clear the smoke.

The One-Hour Laundry stayed in business, to their credit, and always had a few customers who read their papers and magazines while their clothes tumbled and sloshed in the automatic machines.

Mama's business—like those of the other ladies of the same profession—did not suffer at all and we continued our wagon trip to and from her customers' homes for many years.

A Hit for Hanratty

I have often wondered why stickball was never considered a sport with Olympic possibilities. In spite of the variety of organized sports my brothers, friends and I were involved with, stickball was really the great neighborhood pastime, open to all.

Perhaps what forever barred stickball from recognition as one of the great sporting events of all time was the complete informality of the game. There were no real teams and, unlike most other sports we played, the competition remained in the neighborhood. We didn't go around playing other neighborhoods and we could care less about who did what over on Coleman Street. The only thing that was important to us was what went on with the Maxwell Street kids; that was it.

Virtually every kid I knew played stickball. Girls played alongside the boys; in fact, many of the neighborhood girls were as good—or better—than some of the boys who played. The season began as soon as the snow was gone and the streets dry enough to play on. Kevin would run up the stairs of our decaying tenement hollering that the game was on, and down we would go into the street to play, cheering each other on and moaning over the missed hit or the fact that Bloke's run to home plate was hampered by Mr. Donovan's Studebaker.

There were no real rules for stickball, no set number of innings or complicated procedures. The game started when we began and ended when it was too dark to see the ball or when we had to go do something else. Equipment was simple: a three-foot length of broomstick, some friction tape to put on the end of the stick so it would be easier to hold, a handful of dirt to rub on the friction tape so it wouldn't be sticky, and a tennis ball. Bases were either utility poles or parked cars. We used the metal cover of the storm drain for homeplate. The only other requirement was that someone watch the street and yell "Car!" when he or she saw one coming.

Stickball was part of the everyday ebb and flow of the neighborhood. Men walking home from a day at the roundhouse, swinging their lunch pails, would holler out "Who's winning?"

"Dunno, Mr. O'Toole!" one of the kids would holler back.

It wasn't really important who was winning because we were playing the same game we had begun a month before. We may have changed teams a dozen times (in fact, some of us had trouble remembering who was on what team on any given day). But that was unimportant, too.

Stickball was part of who we were and where we lived, a part of growing up on city streets. It was a means of relaxation and fun without the barriers of formality, a game that everyone—even grownups and important people like Monsignor Hanratty—could get involved with.

"You know," Monsignor once said during a sermon on a warm, summer Sunday, "heaven is probably something like a great neighborhood of familiar friends. A place where we gather on a beautiful day like this and watch our children at their stickball games without worrying about cars. A place where our loving Father watches over us to satisfy our needs and allows us to enjoy the pleasures he has prepared for us."

It may not have been great theology but it made sense to us. The neighborhood was our world and everything that made up that neighborhood was important to each of us in some way or other.

In many ways our stickball games reflected our ecumenical outlook on life. Just as we lived and interacted with each other without giving a thought to race or religion, we played the game without any regard for who you were or how well you played. No one had any particular position to play because you played whatever position needed to be filled. Sides were chosen simply by kids gathering on one part of the sidewalk or another.

It was not uncommon for Mr. Munstein to send one of his helpers out during the heat of the game with a pitcher of lemonade made fresh in the back room of the grocery store. When business was slow, the various merchants along the street would stand outside to watch the game. Even Mama realized the importance of stickball and often stopped to watch a game in progress along with Mrs. O'Malley or Mrs. Saperstein.

As fall descended and the leaves swirled around in the gutters and down onto the sidewalks, we began to play in earnest because we knew our stickball days were limited and that snow would soon blanket the pavement and cover homeplate. Then, sometimes only a handful of kids would play because the rest of us were involved in football practice or in doing homework.

One crisp fall day, Monsignor Hanratty stopped by on his neighborhood rounds to watch the game in progress.

"Hi, Monsignor!" Charlie Carroll yelled as he took his place at bat.

"Hi, yourselves!" the powerful pastor called, smiling at our hodge-podge group of players.

Charlie concentrated on making a hit while Maura Skully leaned into her pitch, putting a fast strike across the plate.

Monsignor nodded appreciatively.

"Good throw, Maura!" he complimented.

That was the end of Maura's good throws, for the moment. Charlie sent the next pitch over Bloke's head and rounded the bases, while Bloke ran furiously down the street after the well-hit ball.

Monsignor was rubbing his hands together and seemed to want to say something.

"Did you ever play stickball, Monsignor?" Victor asked boldly.

Monsignor became animated.

"Grew up on it, I did!" he said enthusiastically. "Not many could out-hit old Slugger Hanratty in my time. My sister was even better than I was!"

"Want to hit one, Monsignor?" Kevin hollered from first base which was an Oldsmobile with hydromatic drive that was blocking the utility pole we normally used.

Monsignor looked around and hesitated. Then Maura called that she would take it easy on him if he wanted.

"Pitch as you will!" Monsignor grinned. He pulled off his heavy overcoat and handed it to Regan O'Farrell. Then, he gave his suit coat to Irene O'Donnell. His black shirtfront contrasted with the crisp starchiness of the long-sleeved white shirt he wore. Monsignor flexed his arms a couple of times and reached for the broomstick bat Danny held out to him.

"It's been a long time," the priest muttered as he took a couple of practice swings. Then, stepping up to the plate, Slugger Hanratty leaned over the manhole cover and glared professionally at Maura Skully as she prepared to pitch.

"Strike!" Danny hollered as the tennis ball whizzed past Monsignor like a spring breeze.

Danny tossed the ball back to Maura.

Monsignor leaned over the plate again.

This time we heard the familiar "thud" as the rubber tennis ball met the slim broomstick bat. Monsignor hit the ball as square as any hit could be! The ball stayed in line with the street instead of rising up and shot in a beeline over towards the Oldsmobile where Kevin stood.

"Yikes!" Kevin yelled and jumped up to catch the speeding ball. He missed.

A resounding crash, followed by the melodic tinkling of broken glass shattered the afternoon quiet. Monsignor's hit had gone straight past Kevin, over the Oldsmobile, and directly into the living room window of the Kirschenbaum apartment!

Not only that, when a stunned Mrs. Kirschenbaum came out to see what had caused the damage to her front window, she also informed us that the ball had hit a framed picture of her native Russia and broken that glass, too, as well as knocking a vase off her mantel, breaking it into a thousand pieces!

Monsignor apologized profusely to Mrs. Kirschenbaum, promising to send Finneran over in a matter of minutes to repair the window. He also promised to have a new glass put into her picture frame and to try to replace her vase as well.

That was the last time Monsignor ever played stickball.

"I didn't know a tennis ball could ever do all that!" Mrs. Kirschenbaum said pleasantly, after the shock had worn off. "I often watch the children at their game, and sometimes they even hit my window. But the ball just never did anything like that."

After serving the early Mass the next morning Danny and I joked with Father O'Phelan and Sister St. Patrick about Monsignor's big hit. Father said it didn't surprise him that Monsignor could hit so well. After all, he mused, didn't *everyone* play stickball as a child?

I glanced over at Sister St. Patrick who was busy folding surplices.

She looked back and winked. Then she motioned to Danny, who was holding the candle snuffer in his hand, to give her the instrument. Sister stood away from the table, held the snuffer like a stickball bat, and gave it a couple of swings.

"Enough said," she laughed, and gave Danny his snuffer.

"Slugger Hanratty, indeed!" she said softly as she went back to her folding. "Cleveland isn't the only place one plays stickball!"

Take Us Out to the Ballgame

Nineteen forty-eight was the year our local baseball team, the Cleveland Indians, won the whole thing—the American League pennant and the coveted World Series.

The entire city was giddy with excitement during the last weeks of competition, and the hallowed halls of St. Columbkille School were less subdued than usual as schoolmates gave the "thumbs up" sign as they passed each other in the hall. Even Finneran, the custodian, moved his radio from the church to the basement of the school, so that the sound of the games, from the first to the ninth inning, filled most of the first-floor corridor. Pennant fever was at an all-time high.

Then, about a week before the end of the season, the new team owner, Mr. Bill Veeck, announced that the following Wednesday would be Kids' Day at the ballpark and that any kid under sixteen could get in to the game absolutely free. To show he was serious, a large box of Kids' Day tickets arrived at St. Columbkille School, as did similar boxes at every other school in the city.

"They have to let us go!" Victor Doyle excitedly chattered. "It would be a sin to waste a free ticket!"

I don't know if it was fear of the sinfulness of waste or not, but on Tuesday afternoon we were told that school would be dismissed at noon on Wednesday and that there would be buses to take us down to the ballpark! The nuns told us that those of us on the school baseball team could wear our uniforms to the game to show the world that St. Columbkille supported baseball, God, and fair play.

Regardless of what we assumed was a lack of familiarity with the sport, the nuns were excited, too. Sister St. Gabriel, my teacher, led us in a long prayer thanking God for making baseball, the Cleveland Indians, and Mr. Bill Veeck, the mysterious man who had decided to give almost 80,000 kids a special treat.

Wednesday morning was a wasted morning. Try as they might, the good sisters were at a distinct disadvantage in trying to compete with the excitement of the day. When it came time to leave for the game, we crowded into the buses. Ritchie Saperstein and Denis Tracy were able to come with us in our bus because they were almost as much a part of St. Columbkille as the O'Neills, the O'Briens or the O'Donnells. Ritchie, in fact, played third base for us from time to time and was wearing his St. Columbkille uniform.

Our bus joined the line of other school buses coming from all directions to converge at the great stadium on the shores of Lake Erie. Upon arriving at the stadium, the parking lot filled with thousands of excited kids, moving along in eager anticipation of the adventure that waited inside.

"Sit in the lower boxes if you have uniforms on!" said the usher as we spilled out into the bleachers. Other school teams were there, too, and because of our uniforms we were given the best seats in the house. As we filed down the aisle, we were handed a bag of peanuts, a hot dog, and a cup of cola simply because we were kids! It was as if heaven's door opened and we were allowed a glimpse of our reward.

I had been in the stadium many times before but I had sat mostly in the bleachers. This was the first time I had ever sat in the boxes, so I was amazed at how close I was to the playing field, the players, and everything I considered good and holy about baseball.

"Look, Sean-o! The Sisters are even gonna watch the game!"

Victor poked me and pointed at the boxes across the aisle from us where Sisters St. Patrick, St. Kermit, St. Mary, and St. Gabriel sat, aloof and slightly prim, watching a spectacle we were certain they did not understand.

"Maybe you should go sit with the Sisters and tell them what's going on!" I hollered over to Danny, who simply ignored me and watched the field.

We soon forgot about joking about the nuns as the game began. It was an exciting game and soon we were caught up in the ecstasy of the great American pastime. Crumpled peanut bags and empty cola cups littered the cement at our feet and we tugged the visors of our baseball caps low to shield our eyes from the torrid sun as our team relentlessly plodded onward toward an anticipated victory over the New York Yankees.

From time to time, I glanced over at the box where our nuns sat and marveled at their patience, watching a spectacle they could not possibly comprehend.

During the last inning, when it was evident that our team was going to triumph, the four nuns stood up and moved to the aisle.

"Mr. Patrick!" Sister St. Patrick motioned to my brother Danny who was our team captain. "When the game is over, gather your team down under the stands here. We'll go to the bus together so no one gets lost."

When the game was over and the kids began to mill towards the exits, Danny led our team down the ramp to the spot under the bleachers where Sister had said to meet. Ritchie, wearing his baseball glove on his left hand, pounded his fist into the leather several times in his enthusiasm to show how grateful he was to have been to a real game for once.

As the crowd thinned, we looked for some sign of our teachers. It was dark under the stands but we knew this was where we had been told to meet.

"There they are!" Victor beamed and pointed.

Sure enough, the four nuns were standing with a couple of other nuns whom we didn't know. We figured they were probably nuns from one of the other schools in the diocese run by the same order.

The sisters were gathered around a hulking man wearing a sport coat and an open collared shirt, sporting a wide, infectious grin. He had closely cropped blond hair and looked a lot like General Dwight D. Eisenhower.

The sisters were all talking at once, it seemed, something totally out of character for the ladies who insisted we wait until we finished talking before trying to say something ourselves. We moved over to the group and stood silently while they chatted—about baseball!

"He's good where he's at but I think it's a mistake to have him start the game," Sister St. Patrick was pontificating. "You need to save his pitching for the later innings when his strength just might save the game."

"I'll think about it, Sister," the friendly man said, and turned to walk away.

"You might just come and watch our boys play!" Sister St. Kermit called after the big man.

He turned around to face us and grinned. "I just might do that, Sister. You say they play this Friday afternoon? I think we're free then. I just might do that!"

"We'll pray for you anyway!" Sister St. Patrick called jokingly.

"Who's that?" my brother, Danny, said loudly.

The big man had heard him. He turned and fixed Danny with his glistening, penetrating eyes.

"Hey, kid!" the man called. "The name is Veeck. It sounds like 'wreck!'"

Danny's jaw dropped.

We never did find out how the nuns knew someone even famous people didn't get to meet. Besides Bill Veeck, our game that Friday boasted such spectators as Mike Garcia, Larry Doby, and Lou

Boudreau. We won handily. We couldn't miss with a cheering section like that!

A few weeks later, when the Indians played in the World Series, some of the nuns asked for students to bring little portable radios to school so we could all listen to the games. Like I said, the whole city was in a whirl about baseball.

Speculation about how the nuns knew baseball, the ballplayers, and the team owner faded into memory as time went on. But I would never again jump to conclusions about the nuns who taught us much more than just our lessons!

Nothing Like Home Cooking

Eating out was something one just didn't do in our world. "Why waste good money on food that you can prepare better yourself?" Mama often complained when she looked at the streams of people going towards Leah's Home Cooking across Hardin Street from St. Columbkille.

We felt the same way. Our fare was simple, but Mama had a way of preparing the most basic foods so that they would taste like treats we could tell our own children about. Besides, we reasoned, meals were personal and—like our laundry—not something you let just anybody see or share.

Our meals were predictable. We knew that Wednesday would bring cod and boiled potatoes to our table. Friday was cold salmon from cans, with slices of onion and a dash of vinegar. We had chicken on Sunday since one of us worked for the live poultry store and was paid in kind as well as in cash.

The few occasions when I ate out were usually with groups, Communion breakfasts and occasions such as that. We gathered in the Colonial Kitchen and sat at long tables but did not get to order our fare from a menu. Everyone ate the same thing.

Monsignor was a bug on home cooking. He seldom ventured away from the rectory, where Mrs. O'Laughlin ruled with an iron skillet. Her cooking was legendary, and the only thing that would even chance to draw him away was an invitation for soda bread and a dish of colcannon at one of the homes where he trusted the cooking.

So, when Mrs. O'Laughlin fell ill and was confined to the hospital for a week or so, Monsignor began telling everyone he met about his plight.

"How can I be a good pastor when I'm starvin' at the gates of heaven," the powerful man moaned on Monday morning when Danny and I served his Mass. It was a big change from his usual behavior, when he would begin thinking about savory sausages, done-to-perfection eggs, and golden toast with gobs of homemade preserves at about Communion time each day, growing more hungry with each passing prayer.

Father O'Phelan was equally miffed about the lack of a cook, although Father O'Toole and Father Smith didn't seem to mind fending for themselves.

"Spoiled they are!" Father O'Toole laughed when Monsignor and Father O'Phelan wandered over towards the rectory, muttering together about their great hardship.

"A few minutes to cook an egg and that's all one needs to start the day!" Father Smith grinned as he and Father O'Toole put on a good show of bravery in the face of adversity.

Now, Monsignor had made his own bed, in a matter of speaking. Although he occasionally accepted invitations for Sunday repasts, he let it be known that he—and the priests in his domain—frowned on being too familiar with families and taking advantage of their kind offers of meals.

"We are well taken care of at our humble rectory, Mrs. Patrick," I heard him say more than one time, "but I do thank you for your kind invitation. Perhaps I might stop for a coffee or a cup of tea."

Because of this oft-stated maxim, parishioners seldom offered meals anymore, and so their practice sort of backfired on the pastor and his priests in their time of actual need.

Mrs. O'Laughlin went to the hospital on Sunday morning. By Tuesday morning the rectory kitchen resembled a burial ground for dirty dishes and cups. To their credit, no garbage was in evidence, but we later learned that nothing had really been cooked. Sandwiches had been the most culinary of their attempts at self feeding and they ate them down to the plate surface in order to keep body and soul together!

On Tuesday evening an edict was made. Danny, Regan O'Farrell, Ritchie and Noam Saperstein, and I were just finishing our basketball game out on the playground when Monsignor came out and bellowed for Father O'Toole, who had been watching us.

"Daniel!!!!!" Monsignor hollered, "We're goin' to Leah's for some dinner tonight!" Father O'Toole shrugged and grinned. "I guess hunger got the best of our sainted pastor!" he laughed, causing us to giggle as we watched Monsignor sail off in a billow of cassock.

Now, I knew exactly what was in that restaurant because a menu was taped prominently on the front window. Often, while waiting for Danny or Bloke, I would read the entrees over and over, wondering if they tasted as good as they sounded.

"Savory Chicken: spring chicken, roasted to perfection, served with mashed potatoes and a choice of vegetables, $1.25.

"Roast Round of Beef: served as you like it! Mashed potatoes and a choice of vegetable, $1.00.

"Traditional Corned Beef and Cabbage: lean and tasty. With boiled potatoes and cabbage. A traditional delight, $1.00."

I also knew that every meal included a roll, butter and a "wide selection of desserts."

I caught myself in the throes of genuine envy, and I resolved to ask Father O'Phelan what each priest ordered when I served Mass the next morning.

"Well, I hope he's satisfied with it," Mama said when we relayed this vital information to her that evening at our own supper table. I looked at the platter of scrambled eggs and the pitcher of warm tomato sauce we liked to pour over the eggs and wondered why *we* didn't have Savory Chicken, roasted to perfection, more often.

That night Danny and I speculated about the priests and their gourmet meal eaten in the restaurant.

When 5:45 AM Mass was over the next morning, we hustled back into the sacristy for a blessing and to find out how things had gone. There we saw Father O'Phelan leafing through the Ordo.

"'Morning, Monsignor," Father O'Phelan said softly, not looking up from the Ordo.

"Harrumph...'morning, Francis," Monsignor huffed.

Mrs. O'Leary stood at the sacristy doorway and smiled at Monsignor.

"I know you don't accept invitations, Monsignor, but me and Tom are going to have a nice plate of cod tonight and we thought you and your priests might want to sit with us and share it."

Monsignor literally glowed.

"Why, thank you, Mrs. O'Leary! We usually eat our meal about six o'clock. Can we be over there at that time? Are you sure you want the whole pack of us? Cod, you say? One of my favorite dishes. Do you cream it, like Mrs. Patrick? I dearly love soda bread with that."

Danny told me to close my mouth because my jaw was just about on the floor.

Father O'Phelan was giggling as he continued to read the Ordo.

Mrs. O'Leary traipsed off and Mrs. Casey moved in to invite Monsignor and the rest for Thursday night pot roast. Once again the invitation was accepted—along with a dozen suggestions for making the meal a gourmet delight.

"Do you roast onions and carrots with it? My mother did that but only for a great feastday such as Saint Brendan or Saint Caitlin." And, of course..."We ate it with huge chunks of soda bread, we did."

Suddenly, the morose, somewhat cold demeanor of the great shepherd of St. Columbkille, began to thaw. A spring returned to his heavy tread and the iron jaw creased in a half-smile. It was wonderful to see what effect a hot meal could have on the most demanding of men.

When Monsignor was gone, Father O'Phelan filled us in on the previous evening's meal.

"Didn't you like Leah's?" I asked.

Father looked out the window to make certain he could see that Monsignor had gone into the rectory. "It was fine there," he told us, "but I guess Monsignor felt he could do better for the money."

With that, Father told us that Monsignor had ordered the Savory Chicken and ate two buttered rolls while he waited for it to arrive.

When the waitress brought out the food, she put the plate bearing his meal down in front of the pastor and watched as he poked at a piece of parsley decorating his small scoop of potatoes. The "seasoned garden peas" and the "buttered fresh carrots" lay helplessly on the plate trying to hide under half of a roasted chicken with its skin still on. "Mrs. O'Laughlin always removes the skin from my chicken," Monsignor muttered as he frowned and looked at the plate.

Fathers O'Toole and Smith did not fare much better. Father Smith said his roast beef was tough and Father O'Toole did not touch his "tender spinach" or "peppery fried cabbage." Father O'Phelan's "ground beef patty" hamburger and french fried potatoes seemed to please him, but he seldom complained about anything anyway.

The sermon on the following Sunday morning was interesting, indeed. As was customary in those days, one priest preached at all the Masses. This Sunday Monsignor had the sermon and we watched as he mounted the high pulpit with a heavy tread. He began by reading the Epistle and Gospel in English, since they had been said in Latin during the Mass. Then, closing the book, he leaned out over the congregation and gave a touching sermon on the "milk of human kindness."

He began by telling us that Mrs. O'Laughlin was back from the hospital and was in "fine fettle" for returning to her own private world of the rectory kitchen.

Then, launching in on a memorable sermon about the corporal works of mercy, focusing on the "feed the hungry" part, Monsignor sent official word that invitations to dinner would now be considered acceptable, and that he felt obligated to become part of the family woodwork in order to "better serve you, my loving flock."

"I was so glad to be out of there!" Father told us.

Leah's continued to survive. I myself enjoyed a meal there on one or two occasions. But I did not order the Savory Chicken, roasted to perfection, the Roast Round of Beef, or even the Traditional Corned Beef and Cabbage.

Father O'Phelan had had a hamburger and enjoyed it. That was good enough for me!

A Breath of Fresh Air

Noneof us was ever really sick. Not for long, anyway. Oh, we suffered from colds and the basic "everyone gets it" sort of childhood diseases. Being an all-boy family, we also had our share of sprains, scrapes, and bruises. Danny even broke his leg once, but none of us ever had to stay in a hospital or anything like that. Mama was probably the healthiest of us all. She used to say that she was too busy to get sick.

But one time Mama did get very sick with pneumonia, and we had our hands full trying to cope with it. She had a terribly high fever and was promptly sent to bed on a full-time basis, and we were ordered by Doctor Blum to "take care of her and don't let her lift a finger!" In this day and age, she would have been put in a hospital. But back then, hospitals were reserved for only the critically ill and dying. It cost a lot of money to stay in one and not many people we knew had that luxury.

Tommy, who was a junior in high school at that time, took over. He taped a list to the kitchen cupboard that showed what times Mama had to have her medicine, as well as the times we had to take her temperature so we could chart it on a second page.

Billy went to the Munstein's Market and got as many fresh oranges as he could gather, and he and Kevin squeezed a huge pitcher of the frothy fresh juice. (Billy warned us it was for Mama and none of us should even think about drinking any of it ourselves.)

The public health nurse for our neighborhood looked in on Mama a couple of times every day and told us how to help her when we were alone with her. Mama did a fairly good job of suffering the indignity of not being in command, so we figured that she must be feeling pretty low to endure that.

In the meantime, we had to learn to fend for ourselves. Mrs. O'Malley and Mrs. Saperstein looked in on us almost every day, and Mrs. Tracy sent Denis over with a load of rolls and a pot of stew for us to eat. Mama's friend Mary sent a gigantic pan of fried chicken.

For a couple of days it seemed as if we were getting on pretty well. Mama was resting and taking her medicine like she was supposed to. We had eaten well, thanks to the thoughtfulness of the neighbors, and took turns staying out of school so one of us would be in the apartment with Mama at all times.

By the end of the week, Mama was somewhat better but still had to stay in bed. David took our soiled clothes to the basement and washed them, after a fashion, and we all attempted to pick up after ourselves so that the apartment was not a disaster area.

On Saturday Mama was able to sit in the chair we had pushed into her room. Kevin had gone to the market and told us that he and his good friend Duffy were going to fix a pot of vegetable soup and that we should stay out of the kitchen so we wouldn't get in the way. Tommy told Danny and me to keep the radio on low so that Mama could rest without being disturbed by the sound.

About mid-morning, after being shooed out of the kitchen for the millionth time by an irate Kevin, I attempted to try my hand at dusting the furniture. Danny was keeping Mama company and the rest of my brothers were out somewhere doing whatever they had to do on a Saturday morning. I could hear the clank of the cover of the soup pan occasionally and the mumbled arguments between

Kev and Duffy about what went in the pot next. The soup didn't even smell like soup should but I guessed that it took time to season, or whatever soup did.

I was sort of startled when I heard a loud rap on the door of the apartment. I put my dustrag down and went to open the door, expecting Mrs. O'Malley or Mrs. Saperstein to be standing there, coming to our rescue.

Instead, I was almost bowled back by the sight of Sister St. Patrick and Sister St. Kerndt standing in our doorway. They looked like Mutt and Jeff. Sister St. Patrick towered over any living thing and Sister St. Kerndt was as short as she was round. I actually stepped back a step and tried to mutter "Hi!" or some dumb thing like that, but neither nun said a word. Sister St. Patrick simply put her arm out to push my skinny body out of her way as she moved into our apartment, with the little nun from County Mayo trailing in her wake.

"Do you have a vacuum cleaner?" Sister St. Patrick said in her booming voice. "Where's your mother's room?"

Kevin had come out of the kitchen to see what was going on and stood there with his mouth open like a dolt.

Sister St. Kerndt walked right past Kev into the kitchen and shoved Duffy out of the way to see what they were attempting to do at the stove. I watched her grab Mama's apron from the hook and heard her muttering about a "pan of water with a bunch of carrots" as she set to work.

Danny was hustled out of Mama's room and we were told to stay out of the way. Then the nuns asked us all kinds of questions— where was the scrub bucket, where were the clean rags, where was the broom, where was the sharp knife, where were the potatoes. Chairs, the old sofa, the table where we ate our meals and did our homework were all shoved out of the way, and the windows were pushed wide open to let the fresh air in the stuffy apartment.

"Cor, Sean-o!" Danny hissed, "We better get outta here fast!"

No quick exit was possible. We were put to work gathering up our soiled clothes and Danny and I were dispatched to the basement with instructions to put them in the big tubs to soak. Kevin was assigned peeling and cutting jobs by Sister St. Kerndt while Duffy, taking the dollar Sister handed him, was sent to the market to get a pound of soup meat "with all the bones Mr. Ott can give you," while she continued to berate Kevin for trying to make soup without stock from real meat.

"I thought you just cooked vegetables to make vegetable soup," I heard my brother protesting.

"Don't think!" Sister said firmly, "Just watch and remember!"

The nuns stayed most of the day. In that time they managed to make Mama more comfortable, wash the windows and let in fresh air, sweep the floor, and dust the furniture. The kitchen was scrubbed as clean as Mama would have done, our laundry—except for the ironing, which they took with them—was finished and folded, and the place smelled of a mixture of fresh air, homemade vegetable soup, and several loaves of fresh baked bread. When everything was finished, the sisters helped Mama out to the living room, along with her chair.

"Like making a prisoner of your own mother!" Sister St. Kerndt scolded us. "It's no wonder she's not getting her strength, being shut up in that room all the time."

The place looked clean and bright when they dried their hands and sailed on out the door, leaving us standing like lumps. When Tommy and Billy came home from their jobs, and David arrived from doing schoolwork at the library, they stood in the living room gaping with awe.

"I don't believe it!" Tommy said as he looked around and saw Mama sitting in her chair with a healthy smile returning to her face.

It was another week before Mama was truly back to her old self. But the change had begun on that Saturday when our world was turned around by the two black-garbed women of God who moved—with a little force and a lot of determination—into our flat.

Once she recovered, our lives quickly went back to normal. Sister St. Patrick was the same as she had always been: businesslike, stern, demanding, unbending, and powerfully loud in the class-room or in the sacristy, both of which she ruled with an iron fist.

But I looked on her a lot differently after her "intrusion" into the Patrick life. I think I looked on all of the Sisters in a different light. I don't think I ever really said "thank you" to any of them, but they knew that I was grateful. We all were.

A Canary for Mama

Because we lived in an apartment building we were never able to have any real pets. We had some misgivings, therefore, when Kevin suggested that we buy a singing bird for Mama's birthday. "Birds aren't pets!" Kevin insisted.

He may have been right. At any rate, we knew that Mama dearly loved listening to the birds when they returned in the spring from their Florida vacations. I can recall her standing by the open window, smiling with pleasure, as the early robins and sparrows chirped their greetings.

"If we get Mama a canary," Kevin pontificated to Danny and me, "she can listen to the birds all year long!"

Kev was always fairly forceful, so Danny and I ended up giving him the money we kept in an old sock in our dresser drawer. All told, we had twelve dollars.

Kevin got a great deal and was able to buy a cage, a sack of seed, and a diminutive yellow canary for just over ten dollars. With the money we had left over, we splurged on a store-bought birthday card.

When we brought the bird home, Mama stared at it with wide

eyes. We set the cage on the table until we could find a better place for it, and we tried not to frighten the bird as we all hovered around. The poor thing flitted slightly and then cowered on his little perch as my brothers and I excitedly informed Mama that the bird's name was John (after John McCormack, Mama's favorite singer) and that he was going to sing for her every day!

There was one problem, however. In our enthusiasm, we had forgotten the ancient Irish superstition about a "bird in the house." Basically, a bird found in a house was an infallible sign of the impending demise of someone near and dear. And Mama, try as she might to become totally Americanized and modern, often found herself challenged by a culture that still secretly harbored a leprechaun and a banshee under the occasional shamrock.

With this in mind, Mama stood with her fingers to her lips looking at John, who was also checking us over with his quick, dark eyes.

"Cheedle-deep?"

The first words from his beak were tentative and soft. Still, he had spoken and this gave us all—except for Mama—a reason to smile.

"We'll just have to see," Mama muttered, heading for the door to fetch Mrs. O'Malley, who was more into ancient curses and superstitions than Mama. A few minutes later, she was back with Mrs. O'Malley in tow, who was ready to rule on the applicability of ancient Irish lore as it related to John.

"Hmmmmmmm...." We stood by uncertainly while our ruddy-faced neighbor peered closely at the little bird, who had now discovered his seed dish. Mama watched the bird eating and smiled a little. We began to relax.

David and Billy, who were not in on the gift Kevin, Danny, and I had purchased, looked at the three of us as if we were nuts for even attempting to buy a bird.

"Maybe Tommy could tell us if he's bad luck?" Kevin suggested, implying that Mama should write to our eldest brother, who was in Korea with the Navy.

"I don't know, Kate," said Mrs. O'Malley, breathing heavily.

"Cheedle-deep?" John put his two cents in.

Kevin grinned his sideward grin. "Father O'Phelan says that superstition is wrong," he boldly said. "He says that it's bad luck!" The irony of Father's proclamation was lost on Mama, who still frowned, unsure of what to do about the new arrival.

"Why don't we ask Father O'Phelan to come over and tell us what he thinks?" Danny asked. By now he, like Kevin, was beginning to rise to John's defense.

Danny and I were dispatched to the rectory to see if Father was around and if he would come to rule on the bird. He wasn't, but Monsignor was and suggested that he might be as capable of assisting us as Father O'Phelan.

It was a warm day so Monsignor didn't bother with a coat, and his purple-piped cassock billowed as he walked boldly along Maxwell Street with Danny and me following in his wake.

"Let's see this little nipper!" Monsignor bellowed as he walked into our flat. Mama and Mrs. O'Malley were surprised to see the pastor himself, who bent a little so he wouldn't hit his head on the doorsill.

We all gathered around but remained totally silent as the giant, lantern-jawed pastor stood with his hands on his hips looking at the bird.

"I don't really believe in the old superstitions..." Mama feebly started as Monsignor bobbed and weaved a bit around the cage, but her attempt at denial fell on deaf ears.

"Got a spot of red on the end of his wings and tail," he said.

"But, you remember the old ways, Monsignor." Mama was still trying to explain her way out of her Aran Isle upbringing. "And, of course, we all know about the banshee...."

"Cheedle-deep? Chirp!"

"Ah! Hello there, little bird! You say his name is John?"

We nodded and mumbled. Monsignor carefully opened the little door and put his immense hand inside the cage!

"Hello, John!"

The bird flinched but didn't flit around. He stood his ground on his wooden perch as Monsignor extended a hot dog-size finger to touch his soft feathers.

"When I think of the old ways, Kate," Monsignor said soothingly, "I often wonder how they've come to be. Oh, there's some that I believe, too, God help me! But there's some that just don't fit."

Mama frowned.

"But they say that the bird in the house…" she mumbled.

"For instance," Monsignor went on, not really responding to Mama, "who is your favorite saint, Kevin?"

Kevin grinned. He had never kept it a secret that Saint Francis of Assisi was his favorite saint. In fact, Monsignor had given Kevin a copy of St. Francis' prayer, Canticle of the Sun, which our brother had memorized and still said every night for his bedtime prayer.

"St. Francis, Monsignor!"

The gruff pastor smiled softly, still stroking the canary's breast with his finger. The bird stood perfectly still, enjoying the attention.

"Would St. Francis ever chastise a lovely little creature like John as a bringer of bad news?"

I grinned, too. Every statue or picture I had ever seen of the gentle saint from Assisi portrayed him with a bird on his finger!

John's fate was sealed and we relaxed. Monsignor took his hand out of the cage and closed the little door. John watched him expectantly and chirped something that our pastor just might have understood.

"Aye! I'll come back to visit ye, John!" he laughed.

It was as far as Monsignor would come to making a public pronouncement, but it sufficed to tell us he expected Mama to accept John and keep him around and healthy.

After Monsignor had gone and supper was cooking on the old gas stove, Mama sat at the table looking at her gift with bright eyes. Kevin, Danny, and I watched her, happy that we could have gotten her a gift she so obviously appreciated. Billy and David, I am sure, were sorry they hadn't thought of such a fine birthday present.

The next day, Father O'Phelan, who had heard all about John from Monsignor, came over to meet the new arrival. Much as St. Francis would have done, he blessed our pet and told us how John praised God with his cheery song and colorful feathers.

In time, John became as much a part of the family as any pet could ever hope to be. We hung his cage in the kitchen near our common table and listened while he chirped during our meals.

When the winter sun shone through the window and glistened on the snow all around, Mama would lift John's cage down and set him on the table where he could enjoy the warmth of the kitchen and the companionship of the family.

John remained with Mama for more than a dozen years. Not only did his chirps and cheeps became a regular part of our household, but we liked to think his presence helped Mama realize just how unnecessary the old superstitions were.

The Scroot Who Came to Stay

Dogs were common in our neighborhood. We had several dogs while we were growing up, although they never stayed in our apartment. They would follow one of us home, be given some scraps to eat and water to drink, then decide to stick around for a while.

Father Guilhooley, the diminutive and somewhat ancient founding pastor of St. Columbkille parish, had an equally ancient Irish setter whom he affectionately named Edward. Edward Guilhooley shared the life of his person and was considered an integral part of the parish for as far back as I could remember.

Most of the dogs we knew, however, were not purebreds like Edward Guilhooley. They were undistinguished multi-breeds of all shapes and sizes, who melted into the woodwork of the neighborhood. Poverty had given most of the people in our neighborhood a soft heart towards a sloe-eyed mongrel who looked longingly at the last bit of a hot dog or a scrap of cheese in that human's hand.

"Here, boy!" a voice would say soothingly. The mutt would pad on over and take the bit of food appreciatively, pledging undying friendship and loyalty in return.

These dogs were affectionately called "scroots."

Even owners of purebreds like Edward Guilhooley treated a scroot as an equal to their own more lettered and well-parented pet. Father Guilhooley had the same affectionate pat for a scroot as he did for his own Irish setter, whom he felt was often better companionship than some of the parishioners who sought his ear for one reason or other.

It was a scroot that came into our lives and, from us, to our beloved senior assistant pastor, Father O'Phelan. Actually, the exact order was from Din to Kevin to Father, but that makes little difference now. It is sufficient to say that this scroot was destined from the start to help Father O'Phelan in his quest for souls.

"Where did you get the scroot, Kev?" Billy asked one day when he saw Kevin coming home from his newspaper delivery route, pulling his wagon and coaxing a somewhat nondescript black dog along. We were sitting on the stoop of our apartment building on one of the first warm days of spring. Danny and I had just finished shining shoes and selling newspapers at Patrick's Corner.

"Din found him but he has Boy now that Mr. Twomey died," Kevin answered. Indeed, when Mr. Twomey died, the guardianship of Boy, a tall, yellow scroot whom Mr. Twomey had befriended, fell to Reverend Tracy and Denis (Din).

Din had seen Kevin walking home from delivering his papers and had told him about the new scroot, who had moved into his backyard several days before.

"Dad says we can't keep two dogs so I have to find someone to take this one." Din said. Kevin, always one to oblige, took the short clothesline leash tied to the dog's neck, and that was how the scroot came to be at our stoop.

The dog was medium size and had slightly curled black hair. He seemed to be a combination of setter, retriever, and cocker spaniel, judging by the ears and coat. We knew beyond any shadow of doubt that we could not keep the dog. Apartment dwellers seldom had such luxuries, and this dog needed more than just shelter in our doghouse. We would have to find someone else for take care of it.

"You know we can't really keep him, Kev!" Danny said, reaching down to stroke the tight curls of black hair. The scroot looked up at Danny and rewarded him with an appreciative grin.

"Well, we'll keep him tonight and then see what we can do," Kevin said, confident he could get Mama to agree to board the scroot for a night or two.

The dog slept in our room that night, flopped on the floor between two of the beds and snoring softly as we all passed a peaceful night, hoping that tomorrow would bring a new home for the dog.

Kevin was up with Danny and me. He could have slept until 6:00 AM but, instead, he got dressed and said he was coming with us to St. Columbkille for the 5:45 AM Mass, which Danny and I had been serving since Mass was invented.

The morning was crisp as we walked along. The scroot trotted along with us, looking over the neighborhood and taking stock of everything that dogs were interested in. We didn't have to use the clothesline leash because he seemed to be at home with us and walked right alongside.

"What a wonderful dog!" Father O'Phelan gushed when we entered the sacristy, the scroot following behind.

"Oh! Sorry, Father! He's just a scroot who we found, and I forgot to close the door before he could come in!" Kevin apologized as he started to reach for the nonexistent collar to lead the dog outside. "I'll get him outside right away!"

Father O'Phelan reached down and rubbed the scroot's head with vigor.

"What a wonderful dog!" he repeated, still stroking the smooth fur and making "tsk! tsk!" sounds as he knelt to make friends with our scroot.

The scroot took to Father instantly. We saw the tail begin to wag in earnest and he pushed his head closer to the priest for more of the attention Father had begun to lavish on him.

Danny and I hurried into our cassocks and surplices, lit the candles, and put the cruets out while Father and Kevin cooed over the scroot and vied to see who could pet him most. Father finally stood up and vested for Mass. Kevin asked if it would be all right for him to stay in the sacristy and take care of the animal. Father agreed and we entered the sanctuary, beginning the celebration of the ancient ritual while our brother and the scroot watched in silence.

After Mass we waited out in the garden by the rectory while Father unvested. Monsignor Hanratty met the scroot and agreed that he was a fine looking dog, indeed. When Father O'Phelan joined us, both clerics held an animated discussion on the merits of the scroot, each one sounding like an expert on the subject although neither knew much about dogs.

"Well, we have to go find a place for the scroot," Kevin said softly. "We can't keep him in our flat and we don't want to just leave him on the street."

In the meantime, the scroot was nuzzling against Father O'Phelan, who knelt with one hand on the dog and the other hand on his knee.

"Wait a moment, boys," Monsignor said thoughtfully, "perhaps we know someone who can care for this fine animal."

Father O'Phelan looked up.

"Perhaps the Grassi family, Monsignor," Father began. "Perhaps they can use a nice dog. Certainly this one would be no trouble. And see how he loves people!"

Monsignor looked at us and winked.

"I was thinking more of someone closer by," he said, "We've not had a dog in the rectory since Edward Guilhooley went to his own reward after our sainted pastor."

Father O'Phelan looked up with a surprised smile.

"You mean we could keep him, Monsignor?" he gasped breathlessly, like a child who had just met Santa in the grocery store.

"More like you, Father!" Monsignor beamed. "The scroot seems to have made you his favorite and I see no reason why you should not be the one to take him in."

Father cleared his throat seven or eight million times and stood up proudly to accept the responsibility laid on his shoulders by his superior.

"I will do my best, Monsignor! That is, if it is acceptable to Kevin!"

Kevin grinned and nodded. It was obvious that this was what he had planned all along.

The scroot became a part of the parish woodwork, much as Edward Guilhooley had been. Father O'Phelan named the scroot Kevin in honor of our brother, who had brought them together. He was duly flattered by this unique distinction.

From that time on, Kevin O'Phelan was inseparable from his master. The two became a common sight on Hardin Street as Father made his daily visitations to the parishioners. Like Edward Guilhooley, Kevin O'Phelan learned to sit patiently in the sacristy while Father said Mass or heard confessions. After Mass, Kevin would line up with the altar servers and, while Father blessed us, bend his head slightly as he waited for the affectionate pat which was sure to come.

Several years after Kevin O'Phelan had moved in, I recall talking with Father O'Phelan as we stood on the steps of the church on a beautiful spring day. Kevin O'Phelan sat placidly next to the priest while we chatted, nodding to the parishioners who passed by and receiving an occasional pat from one or the other.

"He teaches me patience," Father said, looking down at his companion, "and shows me more about God's love every day. I think Kevin was put into my life for just that purpose!"

"He certainly took to you that day, Father!" I grinned.

"I think, perhaps, he recognized another scroot!" Father said softly, "for that's all I am in God's eyes: a scroot like Kevin!"

A scroot perhaps. But God never said a scroot was not as important as a king or queen.

Cats in the Belfry

Perhaps one of the strangest "friendships" I ever witnessed was the bond we between Kevin O'Phelan and a cat we called Sally. Kevin, as you've just learned, was the mongrel pup adopted by Father O'Phelan.

Sally, on the other hand, was a mostly white female cat who wandered in from God-knows-where and who was dutifully given a saucer of milk and a dish of food at the convent door. We all thought she had a made a home under the convent porch because that's where she went after her meal.

Father O'Phelan was generous with his trust for Kevin. He seldom scolded him or gave him commands like "heel" or "stay," presuming that the dog would simply do whatever was required under the circumstances. During school, we could see Kevin from our classroom window wandering around the property as if inspecting his domain. Sometimes Father O'Phelan would come out of the rectory and whistle for his charge to accompany him on his rounds, or to give him an unexpected snack that Father had found while passing through the kitchen.

It was always fun, too, to watch the lithe dog prance around with the birds and squirrels that flocked around our playground. There was a single tree in the playground, directly in front of the school doors, and it was the center of activity when the children weren't around. Kevin would play games with the squirrels, who were never in any danger of being harmed by the dog. They were his friends and were treated as such.

At recess, Kevin would trot out and sit on the back steps of the rectory waiting patiently for us kids to wander over from our games and pat his head or let him nuzzle against us. It was his due and we were not above honoring him in this regard.

Sally had been a patron of the convent for more than a week before she caught Kevin's eye. After that, the two became constant companions and it was odd to see the one without the other in close attendance. They took each other for granted and it was soon noticed that when Kevin came out of his cozy rectory, he usually headed straight for the convent porch to bark for his friend.

"What d'ye feed Sally, Sister?" I once asked Sister St. Chantal who had taken her care as a personal duty.

"A little of this and a little of that," she told me. "Sally is always grateful for whatever we can give her and she eats every bite without a complaint."

My nosiness was well known and I learned that Sally usually ate whatever the good Sisters gave her and was not very finicky about what it was. She loved her fish and her bit of chicken, but she never shied away from a dab of egg or a nice dish of milktoast if that was what the convent fare had been.

Soon Sally was spending more time out from under her porch hideaway, lolling in the sunlight with her new friend or following him as he made his important inspection rounds which he assumed were part of his responsibilities as official rectory dog.

"Aye," Father O'Phelan said as he unvested after the early Mass one morning, "they have become close friends and it reminds me of how St. Francis must have felt as he lived in the company of God's small creatures."

Usually, the two friends lay on the carpet just inside of the sacristy door while Father O'Phelan said his morning Mass. They knew better than to enter the sanctuary but we all knew they were there and even Monsignor stepped carefully if he approached the open door to say a few prayers before vesting for his own Mass.

They soon ceased to be considered a novelty and, at least at St. Columbkille, became part of the woodwork.

This friendship went on for weeks with the two friends spending the daylight hours lolling around, chasing butterflies or just conversing in whatever language they understood. As the day waned into twilight, Father O'Phelan's shrill whistle summoned Kevin back to the rectory and Sally went, presumably, under her porch for a nice sleep and to dream of the activities in store for the morrow.

Then, one day, we noticed that Sally was gone.

"Cats are like that," Sister. St. Chantal told us with a hint of sadness in her voice, "and they often go their own way. We like to think they are under our care but, in truth, I think they allow us to associate with them."

I, for one, was not really a fan of cats. I liked them, but considered myself a dog person. Still, I missed seeing Sally. I was not alone. More than once during a long week of her absence, our classroom discussions would turn to her and we even began including her well-being in our morning classroom prayer. None of us thought that was out of place and even the powerful and nonsentimental Sister St. Patrick concurred with this practice.

"Cats, dogs, all God's creatures are important," she told us, "and we would not be doing God's service if we did not show concern for his smaller creatures."

For his part, Kevin sort of moped around, lying by the convent porch for hours during the day, obviously as puzzled as the rest of us. He was not a happy camper and moved about a bit more slowly than he had when the furry white cat was with him.

Father O'Phelan was at a loss too. He said that Kevin O'Phelan was perplexed and very distressed at his friend's absence. He even confided that he prayed for Sally and for her safe return to the parish.

"She's either coming to eat or some other animal is eating her dinner," Sister St. Chantal told us. "I put out a nice supper every night and when I look in the morning it is all gone."

Of course, she said, it could be one of the numerous other animals that prowled the urban neighborhood.

The mystery lasted almost two weeks. We were becoming resigned to the fact that Sally had gone somewhere else. No one had seen her and Kevin began playing with his old squirrel friends by himself again. It seemed as if life would go on after all.

One bright Friday noontime, when Bloke and I were helping Finneran carry large bundles of palms into the vestibule in preparation for the Palm Sunday procession that weekend, Father O'Phelan walked by, nodding to us as he reached for one of the long ropes hanging from the belfry bells. Father was in charge of ringing the noon and the six-in-the-evening Angelus bells. Kevin O'Phelan trotted at his heels and took up his position to watch.

"Hi, Father!" Bloke said and we stopped arranging the palms into piles in order to pray the Angelus along with Finneran as Father rang the three-bell pattern.

"The angel of the Lord declared unto Mary..." Finneran mumbled in this thick brogue, leading us in the prayer.

"And she conceived of the Holy Ghost," we answered.

BONG! BONG! BONG! the heavy bell sounded.

"Behold the handmaid of the Lord..." Finneran said.

"Be it done unto me according to Thy word," we answered again.

The bell bonged and we prayed. Then as we said the final, longer prayer, Father grabbed one rope and then another until all four bells in the belfry were ringing their joyous message.

When the prayer was over and the ringing subsided into a faint hum as the bells settled down, Kevin O'Phelan stood at the foot of the belfry stairs with his ears cocked.

"Listen!" Bloke hissed.

We all heard it as plain as day. The bells had stopped and we could hear the faintest squeaking sounds of kittens mewing in the wake of the carillon thunderstorm.

Kevin was up the stairs like a shot, taking the steps as if they did not exist. We shook off our amazement and followed, mounting the wooden steps almost as fast as Kevin had.

There, on the first landing, lay Sally, white, furry, and very much alert as five kittens snuggled against her, suckling. Their tiny mews were music to our ears. We hung back, afraid to alarm our friend whose thick, white fur had hidden her impending motherhood.

Kevin, however, shoved his nose close to Sally, and the new mother allowed this intrusion, cementing forever their friendship.

Later on that day Father gathered the little family into a clothes-basket in which he had rumpled a soft blanket. Then, carrying the cats down from the belfry, he took the whole kit and kaboodle over to the convent where they were welcomed by Sister St. Chantal and the rest of the nuns.

In time, the little ones were adopted by various parishioners who obviously felt privileged at having a "holy kitten" who was born in a church belfry as part of their family. Sally remained at St. Columbkille for as long as I could remember.

Mama laughed when I told the family of our discovery at supper that evening. "I've heard of having bats in the belfry," Mama said, "but having cats in the belfry has got to be God's own humor!"

A Lesson from St. Francis

The day before Christmas back in 1951 was one of the coldest days we could remember. Danny, Kevin, David, and I—along with a bunch of our friends who were scheduled to serve the Midnight Mass—were busy getting the church ready for the festive evening service. It was so cold in the church that I could see my breath. Danny had his mittens on.

"The water's running in the sink, Mr. Finneran!" David called when he saw the faucet in the sacristy sink running a steady stream into the unplugged sink.

"That's so the pipes won't freeze, David," Father O'Phelan said.

The church was rapidly filling for confessions. Everyone seemed to be huddling together in little knots. Sister St. Patrick had already gone back to the convent and we looked around to see if there was any last minute stuff we forgot.

Besides the priests from the parish, there were several guest priests on hand to hear confessions before this great feast. Our diocese was blessed with many priests from religious orders who taught or had duties other than parishes. These priests made themselves available to the crowded parishes for days just like this one, when an additional priest was a welcome sight.

Father Joseph was a Franciscan priest. Since I was always partial to the gentle St. Francis of Assisi, I was naturally attracted to the brown-robed, bearded priest who was a regular at St. Columbkille when help was needed.

"Hey, Father!" I called out as he stood just inside the boys' sacristy and stomped the snow from his heavy boots.

"Hey, yourself!" the priest smiled.

I noticed straw sticking out the top of his rubber boots, and when he pulled them off I saw he was wearing his usual sandals but no socks or anything

"Poverty, Sean-o," Father O'Toole told me when I mentioned the sockless priest to our assistant pastor. "The Franciscans are the poorest of the poor, just like St. Francis. I've always admired how they really live what they preach."

We learned that Father Joseph and Brother Dismas, another Franciscan, operated a small mission near downtown. He told us how they begged for food and money so they could provide free meals to the down-and-outers, who were becoming more and more numerous since the end of the war. On Christmas they tried to have a really special meal for these people.

"Who cooks, Father?" Kevin giggled.

Father did a mock bow.

"You are looking at the great chef Joseph!" he said. "Brother Dismas can barely boil water but he serves up a good salad and can open the finest cans in town!"

I liked listening to the gentle priest tell about his work with the poor. We didn't have much in the way of material things, but we had never considered ourselves poor by any means. Here was a man who stuffed straw in his boots to keep his feet warm, and who did the most menial of work in spite of the fact that he was an ordained priest.

"Could you use a hand?" Kevin asked seriously.

The priest smiled softly.

"We can always use a hand, but we pray that the hand will arrive full and depart empty!"

Midnight Mass was beautiful. Because so many people showed up, the church was actually warm after a while, and it blazed with the light of the candles and anticipation of the birth of the Savior.

After Mass we walked home in silence, savoring the peace of the tranquil city and the Christmas sky.

"I'm goin' to visit Father Joseph tomorrow," Kevin said as we trudged along.

Mama asked what he meant so we told her about the Franciscan mission over on Woodland. She told us she knew about the mission and said it might do us some good to see how well off we were in the face of real poverty.

"Can you give us something to take along, Mama?" Kevin asked.

She thought a moment and then promised to make a few trays of Irish scones, the sweet, raisin-filled pastries we loved so well.

Danny and I had to return to the church for the nine o'clock Mass on Christmas morning. When we got home, Kevin was already dressed in his heavy mackinaw and stocking cap. Both he and David held trays wrapped in waxed paper and filled with the scones.

Mama said it was all right for Danny and me to go along. Billy and Tommy stayed home with her to help get our own dinner ready.

It took almost twenty minutes to walk over to the mission. I was eyeing the neighborhood warily because the buildings there looked even more derelict than our own. No one seemed to be around on the streets. Kevin and David chatted and paid little attention to anything else. Danny was sliding his feet along like he was ice skating.

The mission was located in an old meat market. Inside, there was a large open space where eight long, wooden tables with old folding chairs had been set up. Against the back wall was a large stove where Father Joseph and Brother Dismas worked in jovial disorganization. Their brown robes contrasted with the collection of old coats and sweaters worn by most of the people crowded inside the mission waiting for dinner to be served.

I must have looked surprised when I saw Sister St. John Baptist and Sister St. Chantal carrying bowls of steaming food to the tables. They waved at us and told us to get our coats off and get to work. Father O'Phelan was seated over in a corner, locked in earnest conversation with an old man with dirty, yellow-white hair.

"Welcome aboard! Merry Christmas!" Father Joseph called out when he saw us.

Brother Dismas showed us where to put our coats. He told us that Father O'Phelan always came to hear confessions or to do whatever he could on Christmas Day when the mission was crowded.

We put the scones down and were immediately put to work serving turkey, ham, potatoes, and vegetables to the men sitting at the long tables. There were even some women and some kids there, too. I was too busy doing what I was told by Father Joseph and Brother Dismas to pay much attention to the people there.

I didn't actually count, but I would guess that we served perhaps a hundred and fifty people during the long afternoon. Then, when I thought we were done, Father Joseph led us all in singing Christmas carols before declaring that the meal was officially over.

Most of the people stayed right where they were.

"Many will sleep here tonight because of the cold," Sister St. Chantal told us, "but some will go on out to their own unheated places."

We put our coats on and took the empty pans from our scones. David told Father that we had to get back home for our own dinner.

The Franciscan leaned over like a conspirator and winked at us.

"Before you go I have something to share with you!" he said.

He opened the back door and led us out of the warm room to the tiny, snow-covered backyard. There, in a little group of fir trees, nestled a crèche made of foot-high wooden figures.

We stood there in the cold while Father Joseph told us how St. Francis loved crèches and set them up virtually everywhere at

Christmas. As he spoke, the priest sprinkled a handful of crumbs on the ground for the few birds who might have braved the winter and remained here instead of flying South. He then led us an a unique Happy Birthday prayer to Jesus before he thanked us and sent us on our way.

As we stood there in the snow saying "Happy Birthday" to the King of Kings I noticed that Father was only wearing his sandals and that the snow was actually touching his bare feet.

Our own dinner was ready when we got home and we had to tell Mama, Tommy, and Billy all about the mission and about what we did to help out.

Kevin had a very strange look on his face.

"What's wrong, Kev?" Tommy said.

I glanced at my third older brother and saw tears running down his cheeks, over his freckles.

"There were some there who were no older than we are, Tommy," Kevin said softly, "and with nothing but the crusts we brought them to eat."

As the years wore on we continued to help out from time to time. Kevin, especially, spent a good amount of his free time doing little things for Father Joseph and Brother Dismas. But that first Christmas at the mission had an impact on me that has lasted to this very day.

The Great
Christmas Cookie Bake

The day-before-the-day-before Christmas when I was fifteen years old was one of the strangest days I can remember in all my years living on Maxwell Street.

We were home that day, out of school for the Christmas holidays. About noon, the old hallways of our tenement building echoed with the heavy footsteps of a dozen or so teenagers lumbering up the steep stairs to our third-floor apartment, where Kevin waited for them with a knowing grin.

"What's going on, Kev?" Danny asked with genuine puzzlement.

"You'll find out, Dan-o!" Kevin laughed and went to open up the old wooden door.

Danny and I stood back and watched while the entire basketball team from Holy Redeemer High School thundered in, carrying flat metal pans and sacks from Munstein's Grocery. Skip Hartory, whose father was the egg man, had a full case of eggs in his arms and looked around for a place to set it down.

"Over there, Skip!" Kevin pointed to the oilcloth-covered table. "All the makings go over there. Pans in the kitchen, boy-os!"

Danny and I looked at each other and shrugged. We were outnumbered to begin with, and we had gotten somewhat accustomed to the eccentricities of the social butterfly of the Patrick clan, as Kevin was called. It was an odd time when he didn't have some scheme or other going; but this was totally beyond us.

"I bet Mama'll have a conniption when she gets home!" Danny grinned.

Meanwhile, Mikey O'Sullivan filled us in on what had prompted this unusual happening at the Patrick flat just two days before the great feast of Christmas.

It had started as a simple conversation among the members of team, about how each of them expected to spend the holiday. Most were involved in predictable family feasts and gatherings, and a few were planning on going to visit grandparents or other family. and of course, everyone looked forward to receiving a few gifts. All in all, there was a festive excitement among the members of the stalwart Holy Redeemer Lions varsity basketball team.

"Anyway," Mikey went on, "then Kev started talking about the scones you guys take over to Father Joseph's mission on Christmas morning. He said that it always gave him a good feeling to be able to share something with people who have less."

It was true. For the past two years, Mama had baked two pans of raisin-filled scones for us to carry through the snowy streets at Christmas to the little storefront mission that Franciscan Father Joseph operated for the down-and-out.

"Welcome!" Father Joseph always shouted as my brothers and I pushed the door open and entered a large room filled with dozens of poor people—sometimes whole families—gathered for a free Christmas meal and a bit of festivity.

We would enter and share greetings with the people seated at the long wooden tables, or join in the games the children had organized over by the Christmas tree. Then, after helping serve platters of turkey and ham, bowls of stuffing, tons of potatoes, and gallons of gravy, we would join in singing Christmas carols before going home to our own dinner.

Kevin had explained this all to the team, and a couple of them decided it would be nice to join in and take something to the mission as well.

"Cookies!" Timmy O'Connor had said with some enthusiasm. He had always loved the smell coming from the kitchen when his four sisters and his mother baked piles of cookies to give as gifts to friends every year.

And so the cookie plan was quickly approved by the basketball team. But then, in the manner of most of Kevin's plans, the scope of its outreach began to expand. Someone mentioned that the county home for elderly people was nearby the mission; why not bake a few more cookies to bring over there, as well?

"Don't forget St. Ann's Home!" Sal Consilio grinned, reminding the team of the children's shelter over by the railroad tracks. Back in those days, it was a genuine orphanage filled with children of all ages. We used to see the kids on Saturday mornings when they walked to St. Columbkille to use the gym for a few hours of rough and tumble basketball during the winter months.

The list continued to grow as the boys began to add the names of families who were in difficult circumstances. Later that day, some team members checked around with their own friends and learned of still more families who would appreciate a remembrance at Christmas. Kevin contacted Pastor Hoch from St. James Lutheran and Reverend Tracy from the Presbyterian church who gave them some additional names from their own congregations. Rabbi Hirsch mentioned the Jewish Home for the Aged up on the other side of the city park. "They would greatly appreciate any attention they get!" beamed the Rabbi.

And so, the Great Christmas Cookie Bake began. Since none of the boys really knew too much about making cookies, Danny and I were dispatched down to Mrs. O'Malley's flat for some advice. After explaining the situation to our totally dumbfounded neighbor, Mrs. O'Malley put on her apron and hurried up to our place to lend a hand. She organized the boys into teams: one to divide the ingredients into workable portions, another to mix and stir, and another to form the cookies and put the pans into the oven.

At first the boys shaped the cookies into round lumps, but then Billy Gallagher remembered something and took a paper bag from the pocket of his jacket.

"Cookies need to look like Christmas!" Billy called, and proudly displayed a handful of cookie cutters—a bell, a star, a figure which a good imagination could make out as Santa Claus, an angel, and a gingerbread boy.

Mrs. O'Malley soon saw the futility of trying to get all of the cookies baked in our oven, so she sent Kevin and Duffy down to her flat to turn on her oven. Soon we had a regular shift running unbaked dough down the hall to bake in Mrs. O'Malley's oven, and another running back with hot sheets of golden Christmas cookies.

Hot cookies were removed from the hotter metal cookie sheets and spread on the kitchen table, which had been covered by a bedsheet. As they cooled, they were divided up into piles and wrapped securely in waxed paper packets of twenty cookies each. Then the packets were passed to a team of boys in the living room who put them into bags marked for each of the places where they would be delivered the following day—more than two dozen places in all!

"What's all this?" bellowed a voice from the doorway. Tommy, our eldest brother, had been given a short leave from the Navy in order to visit at Christmas before he shipped out to Korea. We ran to hug our brother and welcome him home. Kevin quickly explained what was going on, and soon Tommy was sorting and packing with the rest.

When Mama arrived home from her work, she stood in the doorway open-mouthed, like Tommy did. By that time a crew was busy in the kitchen washing bowls and cleaning the cookie sheets.

The leftover eggs and other ingredients were given to Mama and Mrs. O'Malley, along with five dollars to help pay the gas bill for using the two ovens for several hours. Generously, the two ladies told the boys to put the money in the parish poor box so that it would be put to good use.

The following day the cookies were delivered by groups of basketball players who simply knocked on the door, handed over the bags with a quick "Merry Christmas," and went off just as quickly as they had arrived.

The sack for Father Joseph's mission was delivered on Christmas Day just after we had arrived with our two trays of hot scones. We were lucky to be able to actually see the pleasure the bell, star, and imaginative Santa cookies gave to the people who ate them. They didn't eat them all because Father Joseph made sure to wrap a few for each family in clean newspaper so they could take them to their own homes to enjoy after the Christmas meal was over.

The Great Christmas Cookie Bake continued for several years after that. It became a tradition that warmed many hearts—both cookie makers and cookie receivers alike—for many years.

A Present for Mr. Stolarski

I didn't take too kindly to Joey Stolarski when he first became an altar server at St. Columbkille. After all, he didn't even attend St. Columbkille School. He and his brothers and sisters went to the "public," and the only time we really saw any of them was during Mass or at some other church service.

After a while, I learned that the Stolarskis had moved into our neighborhood after Mr. Stolarski had been paralyzed in an accident back in the days before insurance and public assistance. Now he spent his time in an old wooden and wicker wheelchair in the family's third-floor flat.

Joey and Steven, the eldest of the eight Stolarski children, hurried home from school each day to tend to their father because Mrs. Stolarski needed to work. It was as simple as that.

But it took time before I learned all this and I remember regarding Joey as an intruder until I became good friends with the family. This friendship gave me one of the most powerful Christmas memories I could possibly have.

One Sunday shortly before Christmas, Danny and I had played

a long, hard game of basketball at the gym with Joey and Steven. The shower felt good afterwards, and we dawdled around the bright locker room pulling on our shoes and combing our hair. Danny mentioned how difficult it must be for Joey's dad to have to stay in the same apartment day after day after day.

"Does he ever get out...you know, to go to a doctor or something?" Danny asked Joey, who was busy tying his shoes.

"Hasn't been out since we moved in three years ago," Joey said matter-of-factly. "Daddy's two hundred and fifty pounds and it's all we can do to get him in and out of bed."

It was true. Two hundred and fifty pounds of dead weight could be difficult to handle. And since the apartment was on the third floor, it was obvious that Mr. Stolarski had to stay put.

Steven brushed his blond hair back and grinned.

"He's doing good, though. He doesn't mind so long as we can make ends meet!"

But it set Danny to thinking.

A couple of days later Danny and I ran into Joey and Steven after school.

"How would you like to come to Midnight Mass this year, Joey? You, too, Steven?"

Joey smiled a bit wearily.

"It would be nice but we don't like leaving Daddy on Christmas Eve. We used to go before the accident but now we spend the evening together as a family, singing some carols and telling old Polish Christmas stories."

Danny shook his head.

"I mean all of you. I mean you and your brothers and sisters, *and* your mother and father!"

Joey frowned. Steven shook his head.

"Daddy hasn't been out of the apartment since we moved in. Mama wouldn't leave him if the place was on fire! Certainly not on Christmas Eve!"

Danny was impatient, trying to get his message across.

"Suppose we could get your dad downstairs and into a car. We could take his wheelchair and all that, too! We could take your dad to Mass for Christmas! D'you think he would like that?"

Joey tried to tell Danny that couldn't be done, how it would never work and how no one could do what Danny was suggesting. But it was a losing battle; Danny was bound and determined to win.

"Maybe it could be done," Joey said, after listening for a few more minutes to Danny lay out his plan. Steven, who was as surprised as Joey when Danny first made his suggestion, was nodding his head enthusiastically.

Maybe it could be done....

Christmas Eve beamed cold, clear, and starlit. A light snow had fallen during the day and the crystals glimmered up from the lights of passing automobiles and from festive windows. People called out "Merry Christmas" as they passed by each other while running last minute errands.

At precisely ten o'clock a caravan of three automobiles pulled up in front of the Stolarski apartment. Several teenage boys, wearing Holy Redeemer football sweaters, were already waiting in the cold doorway.

Joey, who had been looking out the window, hurried down the three flights of stairs to greet us.

"Daddy's been a bug ever since we helped him put on his suit tonight. He hasn't worn it since the accident but it still fits fine!"

He went on to say how he and Steven had told their father he should wear his best for Christmas Eve even though their festivities were confined to their apartment. Still, Joey said, the big man sensed something was different.

We hurried on up the stairs and burst into the Stolarski flat. Mrs. Stolarski, who was even larger than her husband, was dressed in a bright Polish outfit, suitable for the occasion. The eight young Stolarskis were in their best clothes and were giggling with nervous anticipation.

"What is all this?" a puzzled Mr. Stolarski boomed. "What is this all about?"

Steven hurried over to his father as we and a half-dozen fellow football players pushed into the already crowded room.

"We're going to Midnight Mass, Daddy!" Steven said breathlessly. "All of us. You, Mama, and all of us!"

Mr. Stolarski's protests were feeble at best. He muttered and stuttered as the Holy Redeemer fullbacks lifted him out of his wheelchair and into a plain, wooden kitchen chair. Danny and I carried the wheelchair down to the street where it was tucked into Tim Mulrooney's car. Tim, who was my "father for a day" at the Knights of Columbus father/son communion breakfast, was always ready to lend a hand. He and his young wife said they would meet us in front of St. Columbkille and drove off down the street.

"Here he comes!" Victor Doyle hollered as the sturdy football players came out the door carrying Mr. Stolarski. The paralyzed man had been bundled up and his gray fedora plopped on his head. Mrs. Stolarski giggled as she took off the hat and put it back on correctly.

"You look just like the man I married!" She kissed her husband and helped the boys ease him into Reverend Tracy's car.

"I'm glad I won a four-door car!" the Presbyterian minister laughed as he held the door open. Reverend Tracy, our friend Denis's father, had won this Chevrolet at the parish bazaar a few years earlier. When we had asked for his help with our project he had said he would have been insulted if we had not asked him and Denis to help out.

Mrs. Stolarski rode with her husband while the kitchen chair and the younger Stolarski kids rode in the third car, which had been lent to us by Jerry Zimmerman from the ice and fuel company. The rest of us hustled along the sidewalk and reached the church at about the same time as the car with Mr. and Mrs. Stolarski!

At St. Columbkille, the dance was repeated in reverse. Mr. Stolarski was put back into the kitchen chair and carried up the front steps of the church, where his wheelchair waited in the vestibule. When he was settled in the chair, the football players pushed him up the aisle to the pew that Finneran had reserved for the Stolarski family.

During the Mass, Mrs. Stolarski sat next to him and held his immobile hand for the entire time. Mama, who was sitting near the Stolarskis, later told us that when Mr. Stolarski saw his sons Joey, Steven, Paul, and Andrew come out on the altar to serve the Mass, he had sucked in his breath and allowed his tears to run freely down his ruddy cheeks. It was the first time he had been able to see his sons serving at the altar.

At Communion, Monsignor left the altar rail and walked directly to the Stolarski pew to give the host to the weeping man who had not attended Mass for so long. After the Mass, several parishioners came over and talked with the family whom they hadn't really had a chance to meet.

Joey and Steven later said that this was the finest and most generous Christmas present their family had ever had.

Thanks to the generosity of the football players—and their successors in the years to come—Mr. Stolarski was able to get out of the apartment on occasion and was soon attending Mass about once a month with his family.

As we walked home after Midnight Mass that evening, Danny put his arm around my shoulder. "It was a grand Christmas, wasn't it, Sean-o?"

I nodded because I was too choked up to say anything.

We came to our building and started up the steps to our apartment. Danny still had his arm around my shoulders, and I silently thanked God for letting me have a big brother like Danny.

"Merry Christmas, Sean-o!" Danny said lightly as we trudged up to the warmth and love of our home. "Happy Birthday, Jesus!"

The Mother's Day Rose

I was looking over Danny's shoulder into the Fanny Farmer Choice Candies box where Mama kept the tiny items that meant something special to her. There, hard as a rock and with only the barest hint of color on the tip of one tight petal, were the mummified remains of a long-ago rose, placed in the box shortly before Duffy went to war.

Duffy—Dorian Fitzhugh was his full name—was the friend Kevin could always count on as being his very best. So his death in combat shortly after graduation from Holy Redeemer struck Kevin and all of us with a blow from which we really never recovered. And after the military funeral and burial in the little cemetery behind St. Columbkille, we learned just how much Duffy meant to Mama.

Duffy's own mother had died giving birth to him, and his dad had sent him to live with an aunt. Even though his aunt dearly loved him, her own children were the apples of her eye and Duffy felt somewhat on the outside.

Just before Duffy was to enter the eighth grade, his aunt became ill and he returned home to live with his father. Red Fitzhugh,

Duffy's father, had never gotten over the death of his wife and a mantle of sorrow hung over him. He was a solitary giant who would sometimes ruffle the youngster's curly hair but, for the most part, he sat alone while Duffy fended for himself in the tiny flat where they lived, just a block from us.

As his friendship with Kevin grew and he began to spend more and more time with us, it became evident that Duffy appreciated the acceptance he found in our crowded household. (We really can't take credit, though, because Duffy was so likable, anyway!) He was soon considered another Patrick boy, Mama's "adopted" son.

Over the years I often heard one of the nuns or one of the priests at St. Columbkille comment on Kevin and Duffy's close friendship—how they stood apart as the ones to watch on the athletic field or the basketball court, or any other field of competition, and how they complemented each other in so many ways.

I still remember this particular Mother's Day, a warm Sunday in May when the sun had found its strength after a long, reluctant-to-pass winter. After serving Mass with me, Danny had ventured out on the scruffy sandlot where we played baseball and pronounced it dry enough to play on. So we hurried home, planning to fetch Bloke, Victor, and some other friends for the first game of the season.

Kev and Duff were at the apartment. They were fifteen and stalwart sophomores at Holy Redeemer, and as such, they were not really planning to spend the day with us "younger pups." But we could detect a hint of nostalgia when we told them about the game and knew we would see them at the field before the day was out.

First, however, there was important business at hand. "I'll be back in a minute, Kev!" Duffy said, just as we Patricks remembered what the day was all about and went to fetch Mama's gift.

"Happy Mother's Day, Mama!" we chorused as we carried our small gifts out to the oilcloth-covered table. "Happy Mother's Day!"

Mama feigned surprise, as she usually did, and wiped her hands on her apron.

"Oh my! What's all this? You'd think it was a birthday or something!"

"It's Mother's Day!" we would retort.

The ritual was the same, year after year. But we looked forward to it and Mama didn't seem to tire of it, either.

Carefully, Mama unwrapped the gifts. A lace-bordered handkerchief; a pair of tickets to "Bank Night" at the Pearl Theatre so that she and Mrs. O'Malley could go without worrying about the money; a jar of her favorite quince jelly—with the promise that it would be safe in the icebox for her consumption alone.

One by one the gifts were opened and the homemade cards read. Tommy was away in the Navy, so there was a slight void in our celebration, but he had sent a card and long letter which Mama counted as precious as any gift could be.

Just as we were getting up from the table, the door opened and Duffy came back in carrying his baseball cleats in one hand and a still-moist American Beauty rose in his other.

"Here, Mrs. Patrick! Happy Mother's Day!"

Mama took the rose from the beaming boy. The flower was still in a fairly tight bud and dew glistened on the velvet of the petal. The stem was long and green, with sharp thorns and shining leaves which also showed traces of crystal moisture.

We were a bit surprised, I guess, but not shocked. There was a pause in our boisterous conversation as we looked at Kevin's best friend standing with his hand still outstretched after he had given Mama the rose. The fragrance of that rose was heavy in our crowded room; the memory of its scent still comes back to me whenever I smell a rose.

Mama remained seated on the bench where she had opened her other presents. I can still see her face as she gazed first on the rose and then up at the boy who had brought it to her.

"Thank you, Dorian!" Mama said with obvious affection in her voice. "Thank you, indeed!" She motioned for Duffy to lean toward her and she kissed him like she would one of us.

"Just thought you should have it!" Duffy beamed self-consciously.

When we got home that night, we saw the rose had been put into the long bud vase Mama had carried from Ireland, the one that had belonged to her own mother. The rose stayed fresh for over a week. It gradually opened to its full glory and, finally, gave up the ghost.

For a long time we thought Mama had simply thrown it away. Three years later, almost to the month, we were to learn differently.

Duffy's funeral was a somber affair and we all knew how greatly Duff's death affected our Kevin. To tell the truth, we knew that it was a blow from which Kevin would never completely recover. In spite of almost a half-century in between, I know there are times, even now, when Kev will sit alone and remember his friend.

After the funeral and the get-together in the parish hall, we returned somewhat silently to the stillness of our flat. Tommy, who was home on furlough, cautioned Danny and me to respect Kev's inner grief and let him work it out for himself.

David turned on the radio but kept it soft. John, Mama's pet canary, chirped a hesitant "cheep" and then lapsed into silence as if he, too, felt the mournful sense of loss.

"Red Fitzhugh seemed to understand that Duff is gone," Billy commented. Duffy's father, from his own sorrow, had spoken to some of us after the funeral and thanked us for being friends with his son.

"Yeah," Danny said, "he shook my hand and Sean-o's, too."

Mama got up from her chair and went into her bedroom. We wondered if we had said something that made her leave. But she returned a few minutes later, carrying the Fanny Farmer candy box, and sat back down in her chair.

Danny and I were on the floor while David and Billy shared the newspaper on the couch. Kevin sat alone at the old table but we were glad he was with us and had not shut himself off from the rest.

Mama opened the box and set the lid on the end table. Then, carefully lifting it out of the box, she held up the now black remains of that long-ago rose. She had cut the stem short so it would fit in the box, but a few leaves remained on it as well as some thorns.

"I pricked my finger the day Dorian gave this to me," she said softly. "Pricked it on this very thorn when I went to put it in the vase."

She held up the dried flower and tapped lightly on the still sharp thorn.

"He gave that to you on Mother's Day," Danny said.

"Dorian had so little in the way of joy when he came among us," Mama went on, as if almost to herself. "Up to his twelfth year he must have been so lonely a lad! Ah! I often wished I could take away that boy's sorrows."

I watched Mama. It was not like her to talk so much. Nor had I ever seen her talk in a normal voice while tears rolled down her cheeks.

"He gave me this rose and I kissed his cheek," Mama said. "Then, when you boys were getting your shoes and the ball and bat he came over and sat down to wait for you. He put his hand in mine and thanked me for being like a mother to him."

We had never known that.

"Ah!" her sigh was long and from the depths of her own grief. "He's got his own mother as well as Mother Mary with him now. But, for a while, he was like one of my own and I'll miss him so much!"

With that, Mama put the rose back in the box and carried it back to her room. She shut the door and we let her grieve in private.

After her own death we again opened her treasure box, which she had kept in a dresser drawer in Tommy's home where she lived her final years.

As Danny and I looked at the blackened remnant of the rose, Kevin came over and held out his hand to take the rose. Danny gave it to him in silence.

Kevin, now a burly firefighter, fifty years old and graying along the sides of his black hair, put the rose to his lips and held it there for a moment. Then he put it back in the box and turned to walk outside.

Danny and I hurried after him.

"It's been a lot of years, Kev!" Danny consoled him.

"She never forgot him!" Kevin said as sobs shook his hardened athletic frame. "She never forgot him!"

"He was a fine brother to you, Kev," Tommy said, kissing Kev's cheek. "And to us, as well. A fine brother, indeed."

Kevin nodded. "He was a fine son, too, to remember his mother on Mother's Day."

Part II

The Parish Family of St. Columbkille

The Worrywart

My reputation as the Patrick family worrywart was well deserved. I found things to worry about under the very best of circumstances as well as under the very worst. It was not a pleasant task, but someone had to do it.

At St. Columbkille, I was considered an average student, OK in most subjects and a little bit better in others. Math was not my best subject but I managed to hold my own with a little help from my older brother, David, who was the epitome of patience as he sat with me at our oilcloth-covered table, helping me with mixed fractions and the other mysteries of that science.

One day when I was in seventh grade, our teacher, Sister St. Gabriel, announced that the seventh graders throughout the entire diocese were going to take a general test to see how much or how little we were learning. And on that day my role as as a worrywart kicked into high gear.

"It's so we can show them lunks at St. Philomena that we're smarter than they are!" Bloke said, with some intimate knowledge learned from one of the O'Donnell boys.

That reasoning did not set well with me, and I really didn't believe it anyway. I felt that any particular rivalry with that school could be settled without involving the rest of the Roman Catholic academic world.

Since the announcement of the test had been made on Friday, I had good cause to worry over the weekend and I went back to school on Monday sporting a creased brow and permanent frown. Sister handed out some mimeographed booklets and told us they were filled with information about the test and that we would do well to pay attention to the areas that the test would cover.

I got my booklet and paged through it. The pages told me that English, religion, geography, and arithmetic would be covered in the test. Furthermore, it listed just which areas in those subjects would be included so that we didn't have to spend the next two weeks reviewing matter taught back in the first grade.

Regan O'Farrell, the smartest kid in the class, did not even seem concerned about the test. Why should he? After all, he was going to be a priest and usually got all As anyway. Bloke, on the other hand, had much in common with me. He was an average student who did as well as expected and earned decent grades as the result of somewhat organized study habits learned over the years.

Bloke and I differed, however, in one very important aspect. Where I was a bred-in-the-bone worrywart, Bloke was a naturally talented optimist and looked on the bright side of things. For example, when he got the measles (from me) he told everyone that it was God's way of seeing if he could cram more freckles onto a limited canvas. Bloke was the kind of guy who said he didn't mind wearing tight sneakers because it always felt good when he took them off.

I started out on the right track by preparing for the test. I wrote down the subject areas that would be included, divided them into one-hour study sessions, and assigned each session to a specific date and time on my calendar. All I needed to do was stick with the plan and I would be as prepared for the test as I could be.

As usual, my plans fell far short of being accomplished. I was distracted and tended to put off the inevitable. I started "owing" hours here and there. Besides, when I came upon a topic I particularly feared or disliked, I would spend my hour brooding over the unfairness of life and planning to spend my adult years righting the wrongs inflicted on young students who were forced to take tests at the whim of some adult.

In short, my preparation was not going at all well.

"If you don't lie still and go to sleep I'm gonna clobber you!" Danny hissed one night when I was tossing and moaning instead of sleeping in the bed we shared. I had endured his elbows and his threats long enough and told him that I thought I would probably never graduate from St. Columbkille and that it wasn't fair that his class did not have to take the test the way ours had to.

"Well, did you pray on it? Have you asked any saint to help you with the test?"

My practical brother had something there. I had not prayed for success on the test—only that some miracle would occur to make it go away. And I hadn't asked any saint in particular for help in getting through this ordeal.

I told Mama about Danny's suggestion and she agreed that I should show a bit of faith and ask a saint for assistance in this regard. She was used to my attacks of anxiety and had little else to say except that I would do well to pray *and* apply myself to my schoolbooks.

"It's just like you, Sean, to expect some saint to come and sit in your place and take the test for you!" she said without a lot of sympathy. (That thought was probably in the back of my mind, however, if you want to know the truth. I could rest easy and sleep a whole lot better at night if I had a saint who would simply take my place for the day and astound my teacher with the sudden realization that I was a lot smarter than they had figured me to be.)

When I saw Father O'Phelan after Mass the next day, I asked his advice. "In my estimation," he said me with his characteristic patience, "St. Thomas Aquinas was probably the smartest person of his or any time."

He went on to talk about the famous saint who had written a whole bunch of books that are still being used to this day to train young priests and refresh old ones. Father said if it were not for St. Thomas, it would probably be a lot harder to have smart priests and that our own knowledge of God still would be primitive and mostly guesswork.

Father smiled at me, "I guess he would be the one I would ask for help if I had to prepare for a test like the one you have coming up."

No one had a holy picture of St. Thomas Aquinas but I was able to find a drawing of the portly Dominican in the *Lives of the Saints* in our classroom library. He looked somewhat dignified in spite of the strange baldness sported by the monks in those days. I secretly vowed that if I were ever to be a monk I would forgo wearing a tonsure unless God saw fit to remove my hair in a more normal manner.

I soon began my earnest prayers to St. Thomas to help me get by on this test and not to disgrace the entire Patrick family.

"What are you reading in the *Lives of the Saints*?" Sister St. Gabriel asked me when she noticed my preoccupation with the leather-bound volume. I had decided it would be best to read as much as I could about this saint if I was going to ask him to do some really fancy footwork in helping me with the work at hand.

"St. Thomas Aquinas, Sister," I told her, "for help in taking the test next week."

She nodded and told me that she thought St. Thomas was a good choice.

"He was a great scholar but his parents and teachers didn't think he would amount to very much."

I looked at her aghast.

"In fact," she said, reaching over my shoulder to turn the pages, "they had a nickname for him which was not too complimentary." She smiled and actually laughed a little. "They called him 'The Dumb Ox'!" she said, and watched my reaction.

I sat there with my mouth open and wondered why his family and teachers would call him that. He was a saint, for corn sakes!

"You see, Mr. Patrick," Sister explained patiently, "he was a very big boy and not too quick to answer questions. He preferred to think about them for a while before venturing an answer. So, they thought he was going to be a dullard, a person who would earn a living by the strength of his body rather than his mind. At the same time, St. Thomas worked very hard to learn all he could about God. Then, after many years, he was able to share his knowledge with the rest of the world by writing the famous books that are still used to this day. But just remember, Mr. Patrick, that St. Thomas did the work. Don't expect him to just move in and do your work for you! Having him as an example is excellent, but don't let your own duties go because of counting on him. I am sure he will guide you if you use your mind in the same way he did."

It seemed that *everyone* felt I was expecting St. Thomas to actually hold my pencil for the test!

"Why not pray to him each time you sit down to study your books? Ask him to help you concentrate and get the most out of this study time. Ask him to be your study guide and I am sure he will help you as best he can."

It made sense. I took Sister's advice and started the practice of asking the famous scholar-saint to help me study the way he did. It seemed to be working. Even Danny noticed that I sat quietly and did my homework and studying with less fidgeting and less moaning. I told him what Sister had advised and he said that he might even do the same thing. I asked him to wait until after my test because I needed all of St. Thomas' attention for the moment. After that day, I would gladly share him with Danny.

I slept well the night before the test and woke up feeling refreshed and without too much trepidation. I have to admit that I did have a few stray butterflies flitting in my stomach but nothing like the usual herd of bison that seemed to gather there in the past.

"I hope your test goes well, Sean," Mama said as she planted a kiss on my cheek. "You've worked hard reviewing and I am sure that your special saint friend will be watching you with much love."

I smiled and hurried to the church to serve Mass.

After school that day, I caught up with Danny as we we walked to Patrick's Corner for our evening jobs.

"How was it, Sean-o?" he asked with brotherly interest.

"It was a hard test, Dan-o," I said honestly, "but I took my time and I think I did pretty good."

That was true. I had told St. Thomas that I felt I had done all I could and that I would take whatever they gave me. On his part, I felt as if St. Thomas was almost physically standing next to my desk as I bent over the test booklet with newfound concentration and calm.

"Congratulations are in order for all of you!" Sister St. Gabriel said happily about two weeks later. "You have all done well on the diocesan examination. Our class had one of the highest scores in the entire diocese and we can all be very satisfied that we are learning well!"

She said that we had even outscored the seventh grade from St. Philomena, which brought a cheer from the class. Sister did not attempt to quell our enthusiasm and even clapped a little herself at that pleasant news.

"Sister?" I went up to her desk as the rest of the class filed out for recess, "Will we learn about our own scores anytime soon?"

Sister St. Gabriel looked up at me and then opened her book. She opened it carefully so that my nibby nose would not see the confidential information contained therein. It was as if she was peeking into the Holy of Holies.

"They haven't told us about releasing the scores yet, Mr. Patrick, but I can tell you that you did well."

I stood there expectantly. I knew that as an average student, I stood at around thirtieth in our class of sixty students. I was used to being right smack in the middle.

"In fact—and don't tell anyone this, please—you were ninth in the class!"

I gasped out loud.

Ninth in the class. Not thirtieth!

She smiled this time.

"I feel you have the right to know. Now go and thank St. Thomas for helping you."

I grinned and nodded. The air felt fresh and clean as I went out to the playground to join my classmates.

No Banshee for Me

I always enjoyed a good, old-fashioned Irish wake. From the time the body was laid out, usually right in the person's home or apartment, until the funeral, people gathered and stayed with the deceased, talking about him or her and lifting a glass or two to salute the passing. It was a time of remembering, for singing a few songs, and for thinking good thoughts about the person who had just gone on.

Sometimes, when the recently deceased was a person of some note such as a police officer or fireman, the wake was held at the Ancient Order of Hibernians Hall down the block from St. Columbkille.

A good wake was a time for socializing and for getting together with friends who had moved away. Us kids looked forward to having a lot of good food and soft drinks at the wake—even though we had to wear our Sunday clothes.

The fact that our wakes were different—and sometimes shocking—to outsiders didn't hit home until I was in Holy Redeemer High School. Mr. Michael O'Flynn, an assistant basketball coach, died suddenly from a heart attack. Since he was from "the auld

94

sod," his family proceeded with plans for a traditional wake.

Holy Redeemer was not a predominantly Irish-American school. We had a hefty contingent of Irish, but also a good number of Italians, Germans, Polish, and other students of other nationalities.

Since Coach O'Flynn had been a very popular faculty member, and since most of the students and their families were expected to pay their respects, the wake was held at the A.O.H. Hall the evening before the funeral. Mama and her lady friends prepared most of the food and drink. Deegan, the local undertaker, did his usual fine job of arranging potted ferns and bright flowers as a backdrop for the pine coffin. Several dozen chairs were set up in the main room of the hall, but the larger back room, separated from the main room only by a chest-high partition, had tables and even a small bar where people could fill their glasses for a toast to Mr. O'Flynn.

Tommy was away in Korea, but Billy, David, Kevin, Danny, and I—all of whom had played under Mr. O'Flynn—got there early enough to sneak a look at what the ladies had prepared to eat. We wore our dress shirts and neckties as expected, and Finneran put us to work moving large floor fans around to various parts of the rooms.

The hall filled rapidly. Most of the students from St. Columbkille were there and we waved when we saw our other school friends enter with their parents and look around the room at the people chatting and laughing together.

Mr. O'Laughlin unlimbered his pipes and an old-timer named McDermott brought out his fiddle. They stood on a little riser scraping and tooting away, playing some of the jigs and reels Mr. O'Flynn would have liked. Mrs. O'Flynn and her two daughters sat at a little table near the coffin, receiving the good wishes and sympathy of the people after they said a prayer at the coffin.

I was just coming back in from getting a second bottle of cola when Billy Goebel and a couple of classmates cornered Danny and me to ask what the partying was all about.

"It's a wake, Billy," was all I could think of to say. I took it for granted that everyone did up their dead in this manner.

"Seems out of place," Bobby Nemanich from St. Vitus parish said with a frown, "to have all this going on right with the body in the same room, and Mrs. O'Flynn here, too."

"We're acting like it was a happy thing," Tony Morelli muttered. "I'm gonna miss coach something awful. I'm really sad that he died, you know!"

It was plainly evident that they disapproved of our tradition.

There was a pretty good crowd of classmates around us by this time. I felt a bit on the spot, and couldn't quite think of a proper explanation.

Then Finneran came up and bailed me out. The florid-faced Irishman was carrying a box of something back to the kitchen when he overheard our conversation. He muttered something, carried his box into the kitchen, then came back to where we were standing.

"Come on over here, boys," he said over the drone of the pipes, pointing to the back room where the rest of the people were gathered. We all followed the doughty janitor over to a relatively quiet corner. He motioned us around him and proceeded to give us all a lesson on Irish heritage.

"It might seem strange," he said, looking from one boy to another, "that we 'micks' do what we do in the face of death, but don't be too hard on us until you know why we do it."

He told us that historically, the Irish were among the most superstitious of people in spite of their strong religious faith. Tongue in cheek, he smiled as he mentioned our propensity toward believing in leprechauns, clurichauns, far darrigs, and the like. He said that ancient legend held that if a dead person was left untended—even for a few minutes—until the burial, the "banshee," a female spirit who bodes no good, would come, snatch the soul from the body, and carry it off to a limbo somewhere instead of letting it go on to heaven.

Then he told us that the friends and family of the deceased do not gather to mourn a death, but to celebrate a life.

"O'Flynn is gone," he said reverently, "but he was with us once. We are happy that we had him among us for the time he was here."

Monsignor Hanratty and Brother Paul, principal of Holy Redeemer, had joined the growing group listening to Finneran. Brother Paul looked like he, too, was learning something new.

Monsignor interrupted Finneran, probably for Brother Paul's benefit. "Tomorrow, boys, we'll play the dirges and chant the requiem. But for tonight we'll remember the man he was when he walked among us and be thankful that we had him as long as we did. We'll sing a bit and lift a glass or two for a good friend to wish him godspeed. We'll remember the good and not dwell on the rest until its time…and that will be tomorrow."

Brother Paul was smiling. "I've never heard it told why you Irish have your wakes. Now it makes perfect sense to me."

"In an hour or so we'll sing 'The Minstrel Boy' and then we'll lift the parting glass to a good, good man," Monsignor said softly. "We'll lift it up and say, 'Here's to you, Michael. Here's to you, our gallant friend. May your journey to the gates of heaven be paved with blessings that you can shower on your beloved family and on us, your friends. And may you watch down on us here until it is our time to join you in the joys of God's friendship.'"

Later, Billy Goebel started talking about how Coach O'Flynn helped him improve his formidable jump shot. Tony Morelli laughed about the time we all "papered" Mr. O'Flynn's office after winning a difficult game, and we all joined in remembering the look on his face when he saw it.

"He was a great one, Coach O'Flynn!" Bobby Nemanich smiled and lifted his cola cup toward the pine coffin at the end of the long room. "Remember the time he almost got a technical foul defending Polanski when that kid from Ignatius fouled him?"

"He did foul me!" Mike Polanski said loudly.

The stories rolled on, told by adolescent voices from many different backgrounds. The fiddle rasped and the pipes tootled while Sheila McCabe and Maura O'Malley, along with her little brothers Larry and Tim, performed a step dance. Even the non-Irish visitors clapped along with the music.

When it came time to leave we told our friends that Monsignor and Finneran would sit up the rest of the night with the body, praying the rosary and trading stories—to keep the banshee from coming too near.

We all gathered in the main room to sing "The Minstrel Boy" and lift the parting glass. This time the tears rolled down the smiling faces as we stood united, hoping to ease the passage of a good coach, a friend, a husband, and a father into the hands of a loving God.

Brother Paul wiped his eyes as he prepared to leave. He nodded at Finneran and Monsignor, who were sitting in their chairs ready for the long night ahead. "It was my first time at a real wake," he said a bit sheepishly, "but it is a beautiful way to go on to God."

We don't have many wakes like that one anymore. Perhaps we're too sophisticated or hurried to do it the way we used to. Perhaps, too, we're afraid someone might point a finger at our eccentricity, and there'll be no Finneran to set them right.

But if I had my way, my own passing would be marked as was Mr. O'Flynn's—with stories and laughter, with a glass or two and a piece of cake, with someone to sing "The Minstrel Boy" and another to lift the parting glass and tell about who I was and how it had been with me.

As old Finneran told my mystified friends that night, I would have them gather together to celebrate my life.

And, of course, to keep watch for the banshee!

The Forty Hours Devotion

A lot of Catholic customs and practices have come and gone since I was a kid in St. Columbkille parish. One of the ones that had a deep impression on me was the Forty Hours devotion.

I had served the Forty Hours devotion since I was old enough to wear a cassock. The ceremony included an opening and closing procession; the time in between, night and day, was filled with people who came into the brightly lit church to worship before the exposed Blessed Sacrament, which sat in a massive gold monstrance on the main altar.

Big sheets of butcher paper, marked with numbers indicating the hours of the day and night, were hung in the vestibule of the church. Here parishioners could sign their names to indicate the time they would spend kneeling before the Blessed Sacrament.

For weeks prior to the ceremony, the priests exhorted and cajoled the parishioners to turn out in vast hordes so that Jesus knew St. Columbkille was a parish to be reckoned with. At least once or twice during these pre-ceremony pep talks, the embarrassing fact was mentioned that, had it not been for a dedicated woman who stayed an extra hour in the church during the Forty Hours at neighboring St. Thomas parish, there would have been *no one* in that church between 3:00 and 4:00 AM! We did *not* want that to happen at *our* parish, that was for sure!

During the altar servers' meeting held the week before the service, Victor asked Sister St. Patrick if we could sign up for hours other than the school hours we were expected to be there.

"Do you mean in addition to the hours we depend on you for?" Sister asked.

Victor nodded. "Like during the night, Sister," the English boy went on, "when it's dark out."

She thought this over and then agreed it would be all right as long as our parents or guardians wrote a note giving their permission, and that there be a few rules about going to the church at night. No youngster was to walk alone to the church, for example. We had to be in pairs, at least, and preferably more than two at a time.

We were enthusiastic about having the opportunity to do something extra for the cause, and we took great pride in writing our names in the 2:00 AM slot on the butcher paper in the vestibule of the church.

Mama wrote a short note giving me permission. I tried to shame my brother Danny into joining me but he told me that his sleep was important and that I had better not wake him up trying to get dressed in the middle of the night. In the end, Victor invited Bloke, Charlie Carroll, and me to stay at his house that night so we could all walk to church together.

The beginning of the Forty Hours devotion was festive and impressive. Virtually every altar server who could walk, talk, or chew gum (but not in church!) was drafted into service for the procession. The members of the boys' choir, wearing cassocks with Buster Brown collars and black bowties, were also part of the entourage. Visiting priests and officials from the Knights of Columbus joined in. It was a grand procession, indeed!

Before the procession began, Sister gave her usual warning, reminding us of the time "wrong-way O'Leary" led the entire procession *out* of the church instead of in. That story always got a chuckle out of us but a stern frown from Sister, who was dead serious because it had actually happened only a few years before.

The procession went on without a hitch. Kevin, the official thurifer for the parish, swung his incense pot with decorum and created lots of smoke. The choir was flawless in singing *Pange Lingua* with the gusto due a once-a-year celebration. The church was filled to overflowing, and everything went just as it should.

After the exposition of the Blessed Sacrament, many of the worshippers continued kneeling in the church while others made their way home in respectful silence. Charlie, Bloke, and I stumbled along with Victor and tried to appear recollected in spite of our giggles and muffled comments.

Victor's aunt had prepared a nice snack for us. Then, because it was already nine o'clock and we had to be up and on our way by 1:45, we rolled up in our blankets on Victor's floor, vowing to get a good sleep and wake up fresh at the unearthly hour of 2:00 AM.

It seemed as if I had just fallen asleep when I heard Victor's uncle gently prodding Victor, saying that it was time to get up and get a move on. My eyes seemed to be pasted shut. I glanced at Bloke who was sitting up but seemed to be in a dead stupor.

Charlie muttered something about "penance for our sins" but Bloke only grunted a confused "huh?" as we slipped into our clothes and went out into the cold night air.

We were no more awake when we arrived at St. Columbkille, but we managed to put on our cassocks and surplices and stumble out into the sanctuary where several kneeling benches had been set. The church was strangely silent with only an occasional cough or clunk from someone putting a kneeler up or down.

We knelt there, doing our best to seem holy and attentive. My mind drifted off into a sort of dreamy reverie as I looked at the golden monstrance up on the altar. The main lights of the church were not lighted so the major source of illumination were the candles that flickered like sentinels before the exposed host. It was as if God had settled down to listen to me and had invited me to talk to him!

I heard a faint movement from the edge of the sanctuary and saw Finneran kneeling by a big pillar with his head bowed and his rosary beads in his hands.

Father O'Phelan came into the sanctuary and genuflected on both knees and moved into the shadows with his breviary in his hand. I knew he had to be up for the 5:45 AM Mass so I felt a little less proud of my own "sacrifice."

Bloke yawned but stayed kneeling with his eyes wide open, staring at the shimmering altar. Charlie and Victor were praying the rosary, and I decided to do so as well. I soon lost myself in the repetition of the holy words and the joyful mysteries.

Time moved so quickly that I was surprised to see Regan O'Farrell and Brian O'Neill come out of the sacristy and genuflect before moving over to take our places.

Bloke, Charlie, Victor, and I walked back to Victor's house mostly in silence and quietly let ourselves in. Back on the floor in Victor's room I fell into an instant sleep and, when Victor's uncle woke us for school, I felt rested and alive. We had a nice breakfast of scrambled eggs, toast, and milk, which was a lot more than I usually ate.

School was bright and Sister asked how we felt after our early morning venture. Regan and Brian were "bright-eyed and bushy-tailed," so we knew they felt the same as we did.

"It was really different, Sister!" Victor said. "It was like the church was a different world than usual!"

She smiled and nodded.

"Did you do a lot of penance for your sins?" she asked.

Bloke jumped up. "It wasn't like penance at all, Sister! It was like it was right to be there!"

I said that it was a lot different from being at Midnight Mass and that I felt the hours of night were pretty special.

In the decades that have passed, I have spent many nights awake and alert; most parents can say the same thing. As a policeman—my profession as an adult—night and day were of the same importance when it came to doing my duty. But I have never quite gotten over the almost mystical feeling that darkness brings, a feeling I first had while kneeling before the Blessed Sacrament during the wee hours of the morning.

I miss the Forty Hours devotion. I miss the winding procession, the rising smoke of the swinging thurible, and the lilting melody of the *Pange Lingua*. I miss the giggles as we passed through the main door, remembering the time "wrong-way O'Leary" led the entire procession out of the church and forced Sister St. Patrick to run toward the front of the line, waving her arms like a windmill, trying to turn us all around before we ended up at the Pearl Theatre instead of in the sanctuary.

Regardless of which way the procession may have gone that night or any other night, the Forty Hours gave us an opportunity to learn the power of prayer, to have that indescribable sense of knowing our words and thoughts are being heard by God.

This experience will never go away. It will last a lifetime and we were blessed to have it happen to us as early in our lives as it did.

Compline

Father O'Phelan, our senior assistant pastor, was truly one of a kind, so it seldom surprised us when he got the bug to do something different.

Father carried his tattered breviary wherever he went. One of the joys of the priesthood, he once told us, was saying the Divine Office every day. It was, he said, his link with his brother priests and with *ekklesia*, which he explained was the Greek word for church, that is, the people of God. "Even a hermit monk prays the Divine Office," he told us, "because it is the official prayer of our church."

The parishioners of St. Columbkille were no strangers to the Divine Office. Vespers were chanted every Sunday evening along with benediction. I had always enjoyed joining in the chanting of the psalms, but I had never given a thought to the possibility of becoming part of *ekklesia* in so doing.

Apparently, observing vespers was not enough for Father O'Phelan. I was in the sacristy one morning when he asked Monsignor to let him add compline to our Sunday routine—an addition I was not too keen on, and I'll tell you why.

We kids spent a lot of time in church on Sunday. Most of my friends and I were altar boys and served at least one Sunday Mass. Then, because of our upbringing, we were trotted back to church for Sunday benediction and vespers. To add still another service to our already crowded Sunday was not appealing in the least.

"Well," Monsignor told Father, "you can try it but don't press the issue too much, Frank." (Monsignor had long ago given up trying to stop Father O'Phelan once he put his mind to something.)

"Well, I'm not going!" my brother Danny protested when compline was announced a few weeks later. "I've got too much to do and I'll miss my radio shows!"

I felt the same way but knew better than to protest.

"You'll come along and you'll like it!" Mama had pronounced sentence, and there was no court of appeals for her judgment.

Danny and I served benediction and vespers. That was a given. Bloke and Regan O'Farrell served along with us. After the final hymn to Mary we went back into the sacristy where Father O'Phelan was waiting. Monsignor handed me his cope and went back out to the sanctuary to sit in the celebrant's chair. Fathers O'Toole and Smith joined him as Father O'Phelan clicked off the main lights, bathing the church in a soft glow from the candles and the small spotlights high in the ceiling.

"Here, boys," he said and handed us stacks of mimeographed booklets. "Pass these out. Everyone should have one. I ran them off myself yesterday in the school."

The four of us went out and passed out the little booklets. When we returned to the sacristy Father told us to go out into the sanctuary and sit in the stalls behind Monsignor and the other priests.

No procession? No hymn? What kind of a service was this going to be?

People in the church shuffled uneasily, wondering about what was going to happen. Some leafed through the booklets. Others craned their necks to see why there was a delay and why Monsignor and the other priests were just sitting there in semi-darkness.

Only two small candles were burning on the altar.

Father O'Phelan walked out of the sacristy and stood before the foot of the altar. He turned towards Monsignor and bowed slightly. *"Jube Domine, benedicere!"* he sang softly in Latin. "Pray, Father, a blessing!"

Monsignor, still seated, lifted his lantern jaw and sang powerfully. "May the all-powerful God grant us a peaceful night and a perfect end!"

I followed along in my booklet. Chills ran up and down my spine as Father read the words from Scripture that warned of the devil prowling around "like a roaring lion," seeking to devour us.

After confessing that we were sinful and receiving communal absolution from Monsignor, we chanted the three psalms of the Office, alternating the verses with Father O'Phelan just as we did at vespers.

Next, the plaintive *Te Lucis Ante Terminum* was sung by the priests, who knew the song. After a few weeks we would all be able to join in the song. For this first time, however, I concentrated on the little translation Father had included in the booklet. I wondered who had written such a beautiful "night song" and why we didn't sing it all the time.

The *Nunc Dimittis* of Simeon actually gave me goosebumps as I followed along. I glanced at Danny and saw that his eyes were riveted to the booklet, too. It was a beautiful follow-up to the psalms we had just prayed, with its invocations that God watch out for us and take us into his hands while we slept in peace.

We stood as Monsignor said the final prayer and gave us his blessing. Father O'Phelan, standing in the center of the sanctuary, knelt and bowed his head as Monsignor traced the Sign of the Cross over us. No organ played, and there was no music other than our voices.

Because it was after Pentecost, Father O'Phelan stood up and intoned the *Salve Regina*, which we all knew by heart. The strains of the song were softer, though, perhaps because of the dim lights and the atmosphere of peace which had enveloped us during the short service.

Father O'Phelan had told us that in seminaries and monasteries no one spoke after compline. He called it "the great silence" because it was a time for reflection and for turning to God.

Indeed, on the walk home from the first compline at St. Columbkille, people seemed to move more slowly. They didn't do a lot of talking or joking. We waved casually to our friends and they waved back. But we were all, it seems, caught up in our thoughts, reluctant to break the connection which was made as we joined with *ekklesia* in saying "goodnight" to God.

The Great Toothpaste Debate

If you were going to be a good Catholic, you were expected to do certain things and act in certain ways. For instance, Catholics did not eat meat on Friday. Catholic women and girls wore head coverings in church—hats or, in the event of emergency, a clean handkerchief held in place with a bobby pin. (No one had ever said what dire fate awaited a female who happened to die in church with her head uncovered but we imagined it would be catastrophic.)

Catholics read the Legion of Decency ratings before going to see a movie. Catholics made the Sign of the Cross when passing a church or whenever we heard a siren. Catholics knelt in church while our friends from other denominations sat or stood.

And there was this major point: Catholics wishing to receive holy communion fasted from absolutely everything from midnight the night before receiving the sacrament—no ifs, ands, or buts.

Most of us received holy communion for the first time when we were in second grade. The church taught that we were mature enough to understand what we were doing and thus could abide by the rules. Naturally, much ado was made concerning our spiritual preparation. We were expected to have been to confession and to be free from sin. We were expected to prepare ourselves spiritually during the early parts of Mass and, after reverently receiving the host, to spend time in thanksgiving for the graces we received. We were not to whisper, poke, fidget, or distract our classmates.

Most important, we were instructed that we were to be totally, completely, and intentionally free from any nourishment taken by mouth since midnight the night before. For an altar server serving the noon High Mass, this meant a long, long fast and it was not unexpected to see a server or two keel over in a dead faint during that Mass if he intended to receive communion.

"You can always go to an earlier Mass," Sister told us, "and receive there. Then you can serve your later Mass and you will be fine."

Our questions showed we were a scrupulous bunch.

"If I bite my fingernails, do I break my fast?"

"If I find a little piece of hamburger stuck in my tooth and I accidentally swallow it, do I break my fast?"

Questions like these drew snickers. We didn't think them to be too true to life.

But there was one question that made us all sit up straight.

"If I brush my teeth and rinse my mouth and—accidentally—a little toothpaste water runs down my throat and I can't choke it up fast enough, do I break my fast?"

This struck home.

We all brushed our teeth. In our household we used Dr. Lyons' Tooth Powder instead of toothpaste. It came in a blue can and had a little top that you sort of pulled off. Then you shook some of the peppermint powder into the palm of your hand and dipped the bristles of your toothbrush in it. It tasted good and did the job.

When you finished brushing, you took a swig of cold water and swished it around and around in your mouth and then spit it out. The fact that some of the peppermint flavored liquid might run down your throat was a fringe benefit, not a curse—except when you were fasting in order to receive holy communion. Then, the sweet-tasting benefit became a river of doubt. Did you break your fast or not? If you received the consecrated host and dropped stone-cold dead at the altar rail would you burn in unquenchable flame?

There were two schools of thought on this issue.

The first—held by strict hardliners like Regan, Alice Mary McGonagle, and Helen Greene—was absolutist. There was no "conditioning" or lessening of the fact that you took nourishment by mouth and you were going to have to pay the price. Either you did not receive Holy Communion or you challenged the very powers of hell by receiving and blatantly disregarding the rules.

The other school of thought—the one most of us wanted to belong to—took a more lenient view of the dribble and chalked it up to an accident that earned only a few centuries in purgatory instead of everlasting pain in the "other place."

One spring during eighth grade, a group of us were spending a pleasant afternoon going at this problem hot and heavy. We were becoming fairly polarized because of our intensity. Regan's group—the absolutists—was adamant and would not budge an inch. Bloke, on the other hand, had mustered a group who denied any penalty at all for swallowing the dribble. He had gotten Donald Flynn and Karen McHabe on his side as well as a few others and they were about ready to throw down the "prove it" gauntlet.

Most of us were middle of the road, myself included. We figured there had to be some penalty, but to be deprived of eternity in heaven was a little bit much for such an offense. Still, you did swallow the dribble and that was a fact. There had to be some price to pay.

Finally, in desperation, we tossed the problem to Sister hoping that one of her papal pronouncements would solve it once and for all. Instead, she threw it back to us.

"You all know the rule. You have lived with it since second grade. Most of you have strong, Catholic parents."

This last remark was in recognition that Tommy Kaiser, who was a Lutheran, was a member of our class.

"Ask your mothers and fathers how they feel. They have all

obeyed this rule and have lived with it for a lot longer than any of you. On Monday we will continue our discussion and I will tell you what I think."

I made the mistake of bringing the subject up at our supper table. Not only did our discussion include the dribble debate but it added other issues such as what to do when the clock stopped and you ate food at five minutes past midnight when you thought it was actually five minutes before.

Kevin and Billy were still arguing while Danny and I cleaned up the supper dishes. Mama, in her characteristic fashion, sipped her tea and smiled slightly as I realized nothing had been decided by our discussion.

After dishes, Danny and I settled down to finish our homework so it wouldn't hang over us for the weekend. David and Billy had dates and Kevin was going to set pins at the bowling alley.

"What's the answer, Mama?" I asked bluntly.

Danny looked up expectantly. He had not voiced an opinion during supper, and maybe he was as curious as I was.

Mama was sitting in the stuffed chair, reading the newspaper. She had to turn a little to see us. "Do you remember that jar of strawberry preserves Mrs. Quinn gave me last year?"

Of course we remembered it. Mrs. Quinn had given them to her because she knew how much Mama enjoyed strawberry preserves. But Mama had planned to use the gift as a treat for the entire family.

In the meantime, Danny and I snuck a small dip from that jar whenever we opened the icebox door. If we were lucky, our finger would pull out an actual strawberry. Still, even the jam part was worth the risk.

"Do you remember how I asked that we save it for a special breakfast so we could all enjoy it? Instead two boys I happen to know dipped into it so often that there was hardly enough left to use on a biscuit!"

That was true. Danny and I had eaten practically the entire jar.

"What was your punishment?" she asked.

"We had to do dishes twice in a row," Danny said.

It was all coming into view. She had made us pay a price but the price was extremely small even though we had done the act *intentionally*. I could still remember giggling as we did dishes because we felt that the punishment was a whole lot smaller than the crime.

Mama put her paper down and came into the kitchen.

"I want you boys to be strong and good Catholics," she said, "but I don't want you to be so caught up in the little things that you forget what being a Catholic is all about. Did you love me any less when you ate those preserves?"

We shook our heads.

"And I didn't love you any less when I told you to wash dishes twice in a row!"

It may not have been great theology but we were getting the message.

"God would rather come into your hearts in Holy Communion than have you sit back and worry about a small dab of toothpaste."

On Monday, I discovered that most of the parents of my classmates had given the same sort of advice in a variety of ways. Sister St. Patrick was pleased and let us know that God was not a nitpicker and loved us enough to close his eyes to that dribble of toothpaste water.

It was a "feel good" day at St. Columbkille, a day when we learned a bit about what's important in the eyes of God.

"Immaculate Mary, Your Praises We Sing..."

You can take the boy out of the neighborhood, but you can't take the neighborhood out of the boy. After high school, I followed in the footsteps of my brother Tommy and entered the Navy, and my first assignment was on a destroyer headed to Europe. After a long cruise, the boat docked in France. My mates and I went off to enjoy our first significant liberty. We visited the impressive Grande Chartreuse deep in the mountains, then a few of us decided to visit Lourdes to see what all the fuss was about in this quaint mountain village.

Lourdes was a familiar name to me. I remember going to see *The Song of Bernadette* at the Pearl Theatre when I was still in grade school back at St. Columbkille. In spite of not having any cowboys or soldiers in it, I enjoyed watching the film and wondered just how such a thing could have happened, and why Mary didn't visit more places to work her wonders on the ailing and the lame.

The ride to Lourdes was spectacular, to say the least. The bus seemed to hang in the air as it wheeled fearlessly over the seemingly too narrow road carved into the side of the mountain. We strained to look out the window but hastily turned away when we saw the nothingness down below and the spiking mountains around us.

Upon arrival, a friendly bus companion pointed out a hostel where she said we might stay. We stumbled through the milling tourists and hollering vendors to reach the door.

The innkeeper smiled at our crisp, white Navy uniforms and told us that we could sleep in the large dormitory room with the other tourists for only a dollar a night.

"Where is all this leading us?" asked Eric Bernstein, a good friend and sailor from Philadelphia. Eric was Jewish, and he had come along with Brian Turley and me to see Lourdes firsthand. We tried to explain just what it was we were looking for.

"Mary, the Mother of Jesus, appeared here a hundred years ago and made a spring come out of the rock," Brian patiently told Eric. "Since then, sick people have come to bathe in the water and have been made well. Thousands of pilgrims come here every year."

Eric said he understood, but I was sure he was just being polite.

We left the inn and went into town. There we decided to go to a cafe and enjoy an afternoon snack. We sat at a table along the sidewalk, drinking coffee and watching the colorful chaos of hucksters, tourists, and milling pilgrims walking along the streets of Lourdes.

Suddenly the street seemed to change. Instead of a jumble of people, we now saw a slow procession wending its way past us. Stretchers and wheelchairs were being pushed by men, women, and children whose lips moved in prayer as they said the ageless Hail Marys and Our Fathers of the rosary.

The cafe keeper hastily took our cups and cleared the table.

"C'est temps…c'est temps…," he muttered, glancing at the moving throng. "It's time…."

It was time for the afternoon procession to the Grotto. We paid our bill and walked alongside the stretchers and those hobbling along on crutches towards the towering spire of the Basilica of the

Rosary. As we passed through the gates marked La Domaine de la Grotte, we were overwhelmed by a constant hum of prayer. It seemed as if every one of the thousands of people there with us was murmuring the same prayer in a multitude of languages.

"Je vous salut, Marie…"

"Ave Maria, gratia plena…"

"Hail Mary, full of Grace…"

We viewed the Grotto from as many vantage points as possible. Stretchers, wheelchairs, and crutches were everywhere. Candles flamed out all over, and the nonstop murmuring of the rosary filled our ears. It was a dizzying experience; we seemed to be in a place where time suddenly stood still. Later, we took part in the procession of candles, singing the Lourdes hymn with the other pilgrims, each voicing the words of the song in their native language.

Back at the hostel that evening, we folded our white uniforms carefully and sat in our underwear on the small, uncomfortable cots. The room was filled with pilgrims from just about everywhere in the world, and we smiled at one another as we all prepared to turn in for the night.

Eric said that he was anxious to tell his father, a doctor back in Philadelphia, about the multitude of sick people who put their faith in the Lady of the Grotto. He had bought a little book about Lourdes which he was going to send home the next day.

"Do you think we'll see one of the miracles?" he asked Brian and me. We said we didn't know.

A German pilgrim noticed our Navy uniforms and told us, in halting English, that he had been in the German Navy. He gave each of us a silver medal which showed the Virgin on one side and an image of the cathedral in his home town of Ulm on the other. He said that we must "bathe in the Piscine" before we left Lourdes, and we told him that we would.

Another pilgrim, a blond kid of about fourteen from Sweden, showed us some pictures of his brother, who had been crippled by an accident. The boy spoke English well. He told us that he was making the pilgrimage to pray for his brother's recovery and said he would show us the Piscine if we wanted to get up early and go with him to Mass. We replied that we would, then went to bed.

The kid woke us before dawn. We pulled on our uniforms and followed him out into the mist of Lourdes. There were already a good number of people walking silently towards La Domaine, and we wondered if it was always this way.

We all huddled together at the Grotto. This time we were actually under the overhanging cliff that framed the site of Our Lady's appearance, and we could look up at the statue that marked the place where the Mother of God had stood a hundred years before. Several other Swedish pilgrims were there and the boy greeted them with a smile as the Mass began.

After Mass my companions and I followed the blond kid over to the Piscine to bathe in the frigid little stone tubs of water set up for the pilgrims. I followed the Swedish kid and, as I stood waiting while the prayers were said before we were submerged, I remembered his brother as well as my friends and family.

I was pushed gently into the water by an attendant who held my head underneath for just a second. The shock of the cold water was enough to jolt even a young sailor.

When I emerged from the bath and shook the water from my eyes, I was blinded for a moment. A light from somewhere— beyond the room, it seemed—filled my eyes, and I gasped at its brightness. Then it faded. When I told Eric and Brian about the light, they laughed softly and said that they had seen it, too.

We left Lourdes and returned to the destroyer later that day. Back on the ship, Eric and I talked about our experience while we sat in the galley, drinking coffee after standing our watch.

"Well," I said, "I guess we didn't see any miracles."

"You never know, Sean-o," Eric said, suddenly looking serious.

"Did it make a Catholic out of you?" I jokingly asked my friend.

"I'm still a Jew," Eric said with a smile, "and a good Jew, I hope!"

Then he paused and showed me a pad of paper, on which he was writing his letter to his family.

As I looked at his letter, he said softly, "That beautiful Lady was Jewish too, wasn't she?"

I read the first lines of his letter silently and felt a tingle run along my arms and neck.

"Dear Folks," the letter read, "This past week, on our liberty— which had been so long overdue—I witnessed a most wonderful thing. Sean, the boy from Cleveland, Brian, whom you met at Great Lakes, and I went to the Grotto of Lourdes...."

A Ladder to Heaven

Arthur Wunderlich was an odd sort of boy. He was an only child who lived with his mother in an apartment not much different from our own. He was thin and pale, but he didn't seem to be sickly or to shy away from sports or other physical events.

Arthur was in my class, and he had come to St. Columbkille at the start of fifth grade. During the year, he had not "gotten in tight" with any one group or other. Arthur seemed content to move from person to person, taking a bit here or leaving a bit there instead of fastening himself to a group or sport or anything else that might cause him to lose some of the independence that seemed to mark his personality.

"I don't think so, but thanks anyway," was his usual reply when someone invited him to do something after school or on a weekend.

It was not uncommon for me to spend Friday night with Bloke or Victor, and we often invited others to come along. Most of our gang did, but Arthur seemed to prefer to spend his free time either alone or in the company of others whom we didn't know.

During one of the times when Sister St. Gabriel asked each of us to stand up and tell a bit about ourselves, Arthur simply grinned and said his name was Arthur Wunderlich and he enjoyed collecting stamps. That was about all we knew about him.

Still, Arthur was not an outcast or an unpopular sort. You couldn't help but like his gentle ways and infectious smile. He just didn't want to get too close to anyone; after all, that was his own business.

"His father died last year of consumption," Mama told us. "And he had a sister who died from the same thing a few years before."

We wondered how Mama knew anything about the Wunderlich family. She surprised us all with her intimate knowledge, which she seemed to pull from some cloud in the sky.

Mama said that only Arthur and his mother remained in the small family from the other side of town. She then suggested that we—namely me, because I was in sixth grade with Arthur—invite the boy to join our group of altar servers. She thought it might bring him out of his self-imposed isolation.

At first I thought it was a good idea but, after thinking it over, resolved not to ask Arthur to join our group. I was afraid that if he rejected the offer he might be saying he was better than we. Or, if he accepted and turned out to be a klutz, I would be blamed for bringing him along in the first place. Anyway, I didn't ask him to join the altar servers.

I felt a little guilty about being such a prideful young man, though, and I made up my mind to see if Bloke or Charlie Carroll (who was the least offensive and prideful kid I knew) might ask Arthur if he'd be interested in joining. Before that could occur, however, a strange happening took place.

Regan O'Farrell, our red-haired class theologian, had Sister St. Gabriel all wound up about the "true" location of heaven. Was it up in the sky? Was it somewhere on earth? Did God keep it secret so that humans wouldn't bother the residents of heaven too much?

This welcome debate was staged almost as soon as class started, and it promised to be the focus of religion class for a week or more. In Sister St. Gabriel's class, we generally got a lot of mileage out of a subject like heaven.

"What difference does it make, Mr. O'Farrell?" Sister droned in her patented voice of frustration. "What would you do if heaven were right here and you might be standing on some poor angel's toe as we speak?"

"I just want to know if I need to look up or what when I pray to St. Francis or St. Dominic Savio, Sister," the intelligent, future priest shot back.

"Are your prayers heard less if you're not looking at the person— I mean, looking where you think the saint or angel is?"

"Dunno, Sister, but if it *is* important, I'd like to know so I don't waste a whole bunch of prayer!"

You had to hand it to Regan. He could make sense out of just about anything!

Sister finally shrugged and said that heaven could be wherever we made it out to be, for all she cared. God made a heaven, we would go there if we were good, and we would be happy there forever. That was enough for her.

Regan looked over at me and winked. I glanced at the clock and saw that there were only two or three minutes before the bell. Regan's debate had made its mark!

Dismissal was a welcome relief. It had been a long day, and the early signs of spring beginning to show outside had prompted some genuine daydreaming.

After we put our safety patrol flags back in the rack that afternoon, we paused to joke with Regan about the whereabouts of heaven. I noticed Arthur standing off to the side with a serious look on his face.

"Where do you think heaven is, Arthur?" I asked, wanting to bring the quiet youth into our conversation.

He frowned and put his finger to his lips. "I guess I think of it as up in the clouds, somewhere high above us so the angels and saints can look down on us and see what we're doing."

He made sense, in a way.

"Why don't you try out for the altar boys, Arthur?" I asked, breaking my own rule. For some reason I really thought it might be nice to have him become "one of the boys."

Arthur blinked back to reality. "Oh, I might. Thanks for asking." With that, he turned and walked off.

We looked after him and shrugged. If he didn't want to be part of the group it wasn't our fault.

The very next day, we saw how independent Arthur really was!

Off in back of the schoolyard, there was a giant incinerator where virtually all of the burnable trash generated in the school was deposited. The incinerator was almost as large as an average garage, only it was made of red brick and didn't have a door large enough for a car to drive through. Sprouting through the roof of this brick square building was a tall chimney—a smokestack—which was as big around as a silo and looked to be about a thousand feet high. (In truth, it was probably only fifty or sixty feet tall.)

For reasons known only to God and the chimney builder, there were metal rungs sticking out of the chimney's sides. They began at the roof of the incinerator and continued up the length of the chimney in equally spaced increments, all the way up to the very top, where tall, fearsome lightning rods were fastened.

At recess on this particular day, a large group of us kids stood gathered around the base of the incinerator, necks craned looking up. Our attention was riveted to the tiny figure of a boy positioned just past the halfway mark of the chimney. Rung by rung, step by step, he moved without hesitation, but we could see the effort beginning to show and worried that Arthur—because that's who it was—just might not have the strength to finish his climb.

"Look at him, Sean-o!" Danny had come over to me and stood looking up like the rest of us. Bloke, Victor, and Regan stood back by the school building so they could see better.

Defying the fear that I knew he must be feeling, Arthur continued up the high chimney. The spring breezes made his light jacket billow out; I wondered if a gust might just blow the frail kid off the stack.

"What's the fuss about there?" boomed Sister St. Patrick.

I tried to slide out of the way. Danny had already melted into the crowd, away from the powerful nun. But her hand plunked down firmly on my shoulder. No escape was possible.

"I said, what's the commotion about, Mr. Patrick? You aren't deaf now, are you?"

There was no getting away from it.

"Arthur's climbing up the chimney," I muttered.

"*Mr. Wunderlich*!" she bellowed.

Arthur must have been too high to hear her or else he ignored the shout. He continued to climb and was now almost at the top. Sister had released me but I stood transfixed, staring as the skinny kid who never did anything reached the top.

We couldn't make out exactly what Arthur did at the top of the chimney. He did something, though, and then began to climb back down. It took almost as long for Arthur to descend the chimney as it had taken for him to climb it. The wind was tearing at him and a couple of times his foot slipped a bit. He caught himself, though, and continued down, undaunted.

When he finally reached the roof of the incinerator, Sister sent Kevin and Duffy up to make sure Arthur was okay. Then, easing him over the edge of the roof, the two eighth-graders held his thin arms and lowered him to the ground where Sister St. Patrick, Sister St. Gabriel, and Sister St. Kermit waited.

"He's gonna get clobbered!" Bloke hissed to me. "Dead in his shoes!" I muttered knowingly.

"Why?" was the only question Sister St. Patrick asked.

Arthur seemed unafraid—unlike the rest of us who had heard that tone of voice before. (In fact, even Sister St. Kermit, the principal, gave ground when Sister St. Patrick took command.)

"I needed to put a note up high, Sister. High enough so's my dad and my sister could read it."

Arthur told the nuns that there were things he had wanted to say to his father and his sister that he had not had a chance to say while they were alive. Now that they were gone he felt alone, incomplete, and afraid. So he had written a note to them, telling them what was on his mind and in his heart.

Of course, Arthur didn't use those words, but the meaning of his climb was clear. After considering our discussion about heaven in class the day before, Arthur had decided that he needed to get to the highest place around and put his note there, so his father and his sister would be sure to see it and read it.

It wasn't exactly good theology, but then I remembered how Reverend Tracy used to attach little prayers and notes to a kite string and watch the wind send them scurrying up the string, into God's waiting hands.

Sister St. Patrick stood with her mighty hands on her hips while the other sisters smiled and looked away. Brian O'Neill and Victor went over and put their arms around Arthur's shoulders and told Sister they would help him clean up after his grimy climb. She shook her head, turned on her heels, and started to walk away.

Sister took about a half-dozen steps, then turned around to face the boy.

"I'm sure they'll see it, Mr. Wunderlich. They'll not miss it where you've put it. Only the next time, just pray a little louder and keep your feet on the ground!" Arthur nodded his head and grinned.

The climb must have been an act of closure for Arthur, a chance for a bit of communication that healed a part of his life and allowed him to begin anew. He joined our altar servers group and began to take part in some activities. One day he even brought his stamp collection to school to share with us. We never knew that collecting such things could be so interesting and fun.

"Do you think Arthur's daddy and sister read his note?" I asked Mama a few days after the great event.

"I have no doubt about that," she said, smiling at the way I asked the question. "What do you think, Sean?"

"They couldn't miss it way up there!" I replied confidently.

The Blessing Tree

It was the week after Easter during the year I was in seventh grade. I had arrived at St. Columbkille to serve the 5:45 AM Mass, and what I saw made me stop dead in my tracks.

There, in the center of the garden between the church and the rectory, was a giant cross, barely visible in the darkness of the early morning. The cross was perhaps ten feet tall, made of stout lumber, and it seemed to be painted a sort of black. It towered over the smaller trees and looked somewhat ominous as the first rays of the cold morning sun began to lighten up the sky.

After Mass I was about to ask Father Guilhooley about the big cross in the garden, but Mrs. Fahey beat me to it. The 5:45 AM regular, who was a washerwoman like Mama, stood with her hands on her hips, demanding to know who had put the cross there.

Apparently, Father had not seen it yet. He put on his coat and whistled to Edward, his faithful Irish setter, to tag along. We all hurried out into the garden and joined a growing group of parishioners, the priests, a few nuns, and my brother Kevin hovering around the strange sight.

"Might be them KKK-ers or something," Mr. Bilinski, the dry cleaner, said loudly. "Put up crosses and then set fire to 'em," he commented to no one, "wearing their bedsheets and hoods...."

Father O'Phelan and Monsignor Hanratty stood silently contemplating the strange addition to the garden. Monsignor rubbed his hand over the smooth surface. "This is finished wood," he said, "and no one's going to set fire to something like this."

I could see that the cross was stained a dark color, which I had taken for black in the darkness of the early morning.

Finneran came over and pushed against the cross. It did not budge. Evidently, whoever put the cross in the garden intended for it to remain there.

"Solid, it is," the old janitor mumbled.

So the cross stayed where it was. No one admitted putting it up, and no one seemed inclined to ask around about it. It was there and that was that.

On the Second Sunday after Easter, Danny and I were hurrying to the sacristy for the early Mass. As we had been doing all week long, we glanced at the imposing cross set in the garden.

"Look, Sean-o!" Danny stopped and pointed to something white fluttering on one of the crossbeams of the big, wooden cross.

It was too high to reach, but I could see that it was a piece of white paper, folded in half and nailed securely to the wooden arm of the cross. Over against one of the stone benches in the garden leaned a small stepladder. On the bench was a peck basket which contained a hammer and a paper sack of nails.

Since it was a Sunday, there were more parishioners than just the weekday regulars at the 5:45 AM Mass. After the service, just about everyone there gathered around the cross—the parishioners, the servers, the priests, all of the nuns, and Edward, the dog. Finneran took the ladder and put it against the cross so Father O'Phelan could climb up and see what was on the piece of paper.

"'Thank you for the success of my husband's operation,'" Father read aloud. That was all it said. No name, nothing to identify the writer—simply a "thank you" for a blessing received.

Father O'Phelan related this story at the seven o'clock Mass that morning. Monsignor, who was preaching the sermons at all the other Masses, also told the parish about the cross, the message, and the basket with the old hammer and sack of nails. He asked whomever was responsible for any of it to come see him and tell him why they did it.

But no one ever came forward. The cross remained and notes expressing thanks for blessings received continued to be nailed to the stained wood.

Strangely, there were never any notes that asked for something. All the brief messages were "thank yous."

"Thank you for my new job!"

"Thank you for John's grades in school!"

"Thank you for my healthy grandchildren!"

"Thank you for our mother's new glasses!"

After a while no one seemed to feel self-conscious about picking up the hammer and a nail and attaching their blessing to the cross. There was an honor system in place with the expectation that one did not go up to see what someone else had written while the person was still there. It didn't matter if you read the note anonymously; it just wasn't right to be nosy about who wrote what.

As time wore on, some blessings broke free from their nails and floated down to the ground. These were gathered up and the empty nails removed by Finneran to make room for new blessings.

Sister St. Gabriel, my seventh-grade teacher, and Sister St. Patrick both talked to their classes about the Blessing Tree, as the cross was now being called.

"What better place to show our blessings than the image of the instrument where our blessings were won!" Sister St. Gabriel told us. All of the sisters were encouraging their classes to count their blessings and attach them to the Blessing Tree.

Oddly enough, speculation about the origin of our cross stopped soon after it appeared. At first, everyone had seemed terribly preoccupied with knowing who had put the cross in the garden. Some had even tried to figure out who had the ability to build such a cross, who might have had an old hammer to spare and who could have put the cross in the ground without being noticed by anyone in the rectory. All of that seemed unimportant now. The cross was there, blessings were being tacked on to it, and that was that.

As the weeks passed and the weather warmed, sunlight flooded the little garden and illuminated the Blessing Tree. It became a common sight to see someone on their way to Mass pause, pull a piece of paper from a pocket, and nail it to the cross. The dark wood was soon covered with fluttering papers, front and back, from the foot to the topmost part.

"I never knew there could be so many blessings!" I said to Father O'Phelan after Mass one day, as we stood on the walkway looking at the cross.

"That's just the blessings from those who remembered to say thank you, Sean-o!" Father grinned. "Can you imagine how many there would be if we all counted our blessings and put them up, one by one, on that cross?"

I thought about it and grinned in astonishment.

"There probably wouldn't be enough room for them all!" I said.

Over time, we began to take the Blessing Tree for granted as it stood in somber glory in the center of the garden.

Then one day, it was gone!

Danny noticed it first. We were on our way to serve Father Guilhooley's early Mass on the feast of Pentecost. The sun was rising earlier now and the first rays of light were beginning to bathe the garden in a soft, yellowish haze as we approached.

"Where's the Blessing Tree, Sean-o?" Danny grabbed my jacket sleeve and tugged me after him.

I had no idea where the cross was, but indeed it was gone—completely gone. Even the hole in the ground had been covered over, enough so that you had to look very closely to even see where our Blessing Tree had been.

We asked Father Guilhooley where the cross had gone, but he hadn't even noticed that it was no longer there. "Gone. Just like it came, in the mystery of night!" Father Guilhooley didn't seem overly upset, just a bit mystified about the missing cross.

Throughout the day, parishioners came into the sacristy or went over to the rectory to ask if anyone knew what had become of the cross. None of the priests would own up to any knowledge of what might have happened to it. Finneran bluntly said he didn't know and really did not care about the missing cross.

In school, we talked about the Blessing Tree for a good part of the week. Sister St. Gabriel said it had been a nice thing, but we didn't really need the cross to remind us to count our blessings and be thankful for them.

The next Sunday Monsignor again preached at all the Masses. He mounted the pulpit with a slight smile and looked out over his parishioners.

"My good people!" he began, as always.

The he launched into a sermon that pretty much echoed the words spoken by my teacher. He mentioned it was good to be reminded once in a while that we should be thankful for our blessings, but that we also should feel a little ashamed at ourselves for not having recognized the need for thankfulness.

"I'd like to share a few of the notes with you," the iron-jawed pastor said, holding a handful of little white papers.

"For my cure from illness…," he said as he read from the first one. "For my husband's new job…," read the second.

Thanksgiving for jobs, health, grades (mine), and the like ensued. Monsignor read a half-dozen or so more, then reached for another small stack of the papers. He carefully unfolded one and read, "For the sunshine in the morning…." Choosing another, he looked out at the parish and smiled. "For the smell of the new grass…," he continued. "For the song of the robin near my apartment window…."

Monsignor paused to let the words sink in.

"We have even begun to remember that even the smallest blessings we so often take for granted—the song of a robin or the warmth of new sunlight—are gifts from our loving Father, too! Yes," he went on softly, "it was nice to have our Blessing Tree. It was a reminder to be thankful for all that we have."

He put the papers down on the pulpit and fixed the congregation with his steel-blue eyes.

"Does the fact that the Blessing Tree is gone mean that we are no longer thankful? That we no longer have blessings?"

Several parishioners shook their heads.

"No, I think not," Monsignor said. "We could erect another Blessing Tree but it is necessary? Again, I think not. Whoever put up the cross in the first place did so because he or she knew what your reaction would be. I think the donor of our Blessing Tree was treated to exactly what he or she expected. And for that, we too are blessed. Indeed, another blessing has been added to our tree even though it is not there to see."

Mr. Bachman looked up at the pastor and smiled his agreement.

"Let us carry the memory of our Blessing Tree in our hearts!" Monsignor said with a wide smile. "And let us truly know how blessed we all are!"

The maker of the Blessing Tree forever remained a mystery. Many thought that Monsignor himself was the culprit. He denied it vigorously as did the rest of the priests.

Finneran, our ageless, irascible, and totally unpredictable janitor, was likewise a suspect because of his skill with tools and wood.

"Balderdash!" he would mutter when someone approached him with the possibility that he was the maker of the Tree.

It was rumored that some parishioners had scoured garages, sheds, and the trashbins searching for some evidence of the cross-maker's identity.

But it was never to be made known.

Even Sister St. Gabriel was moved to comment. "Don't suppose we'll ever really know," she said in class when Regan O'Farrell asked if she knew who made the Blessing Tree, "but does it matter? I think the fact that we learned to count our blessings is more important than who made a rack to hang them on."

Regan nodded and raised his hand again.

"What is it, Mr. O'Farrell?" Sister turned back from the board.

"Sister, does God count the blessings he gives us and mark them down in some sort of record?"

She put her chalk down and walked over to the red-haired boy.

"I don't know, Mr. O'Farrell," she said, putting her hand on Regan's shoulder, "because I only see one blessing in this room."

"What's that, Sister?" Regan asked.

"All of us," she said with a smile, "we are all a blessing, Mr. O'Farrell. Why would God want to count any farther?"

We all grinned back. It was sort of nice to be considered a blessing. We even began to understand what she meant, just being able to say "Thanks!" for the bounty we knew we had.

The Carver's Hand

St. Columbkille church had some pretty impressive artwork in the form of wood carving, thanks to Mr. McNeeley who had been one of the first parishioners. Mr. McNeeley had put a lot of time into carving decorative scrolls on the confessionals, the baptismal font, and many other places as the church was being built. For the occasion of the fiftieth anniversary of the parish, he carved a beautiful screen to cover the organ pipes in the rear of the church, as well as the massive pulpit—his crowning glory—from which God's word was read.

One of the true artistic treasures of the parish, however, was a carved piece that hardly anyone ever noticed. It was tucked into a place of darkness, and you had to know where to look in order to see it. Even then, it was difficult to make out the form in the dim light.

The reason I knew about it was because I had helped put it there.

I don't remember the man's name. It was a long name, with mostly consonants, that none of us could pronounce. So we always referred to him as "Mr. B."

"Mr. B." owned of the most unique shops in the area. It was

around the corner from the drug store, on a side street, and it was so tiny you couldn't even go very far inside when Mr. B. was there. Mama said it was a fix-it shop, and that Mr. B. worked on all sorts of broken items and usually fixed them good as new.

There were always odds and ends for sale in the store—cards with fancy buttons, little ceramic figurines, a piece of polished silverware with no mates, things like that. There was also a little shelf in the store that held several animals on it, each carved from fine, tight-grained wood. It was obvious the carver was as skilled as old McNeeley.

One day, as I stood looking in the window, admiring the trinkets displayed there, I learned that it was Mr. B. who carved the wooden animals. He was sitting on a backless kitchen chair in the store, a look of intense concentration on his face as his sharp penknife flicked and bit and jabbed at a flake of wood. From time to time he would hold the block of wood up to the light, examine his progress, then go back to his carving. Once or twice he glanced over in my direction. He saw me watching but acted as if I wasn't there.

For some reason I didn't say anything to my friends, or to my brothers or Mama.

Mr. B. was a fixture in the neighborhood, and, like all of our fixtures, was someone (or something) whose presence we took for granted and never bothered to question. So it was no surprise, therefore, that I was somewhat taken aback the day I saw Mr. B. sitting in the back of St. Columbkille Church in mid-afternoon, when I had been sent to fetch some holy water to fill the classroom fonts.

At first I didn't recognize him because the old man usually wore a hat when he was in his shop. He seemed to be staring off into space, not really looking at anything even though he was facing the sanctuary. Nor did he pay me any mind as I clopped down the long aisle with my jug to fetch the holy water from the baptistry.

I filled up my jug and came back down the aisle. Mr. B. was still sitting there, looking as if he had not moved a muscle.

What surprised me the most was that Mr. B. must be a Catholic. I had never seen him in church at all before that day.

It turned out that this would not be the last time I would see him in church. After that first day, not only me but several of my friends and my brother Danny also noticed Mr. B. in church, sitting in the back where I had first seen him. He never said anything or did anything. We presumed he must be praying because that's what you did in church. But none of us ever had the gumption to ask.

"That's man's life is certainly none of your business!" Mama told us emphatically when Danny and I talked about Mr. B. at supper one evening. Kevin told Mama that Danny and I were just being ourselves, and giggled when that earned another admonition from her about minding our own business. We glared at Kevin who went on eating, smiling that his point had been taken.

Father O'Phelan was of little help when after the early Mass one morning Danny mentioned the mysterious visitor. Father said that he had noticed him, too—always late in the day, and never there for Mass.

"Do you think he's a Catholic, Father?" I asked.

"I think so, Sean-o," Father replied, "but he doesn't seem to want to talk to anyone. I said hello to him the other day and he nodded, then turned away. It was quite evident he preferred to be left to himself."

Several weeks passed and we began to take Mr. B.'s presence for granted. We still saw him occasionally sitting in the back of the church. At other times we saw him walking either toward the church or back toward his little shop. But he paid us little attention and we respected his aloofness.

Then one day all that changed.

On a still bright, balmy Friday evening a good two months after I had first observed Mr. B. in his back pew, Danny and I arrived at church to serve the weekly Novena of the Sorrowful Mother and Benediction of the Blessed Sacrament. It was almost seven o'clock in the evening, but the long summer days made it seem like mid-afternoon. It felt good to be alive as we entered the cool vestibule.

It turned out we were not alone in there, as we heard someone laughing and talking rapidly with a heavy foreign accent.

Danny and I turned at the same time and saw Father O'Phelan standing with old Mr. B. over in the shadow of the pamphlet rack. Father had a large smile on his face, and Mr. B. was talking at a mile a minute.

"We're about to have our novena and benediction," Father said, "why don't you stay for that too?"

The old man nodded, and grinning, entered the church and took his customary place in the last pew.

Our puzzlement was more than evident as we went back to the sacristy with Father O'Phelan but he acted as if nothing had happened. Several times Danny or I attempted to ask him what had happened, but we didn't. And since he had not volunteered a single word to ease our mystification, we felt somewhat left out. We plodded home after the service, feeling insulted and put-upon.

After that day, when I looked in the window of the tiny fix-it shop, it appeared that nothing had really changed. The buttons, the ribbons, and the doodads were still in their places. The tiny carved animals were still on their shelf. And the proprietor still sat on his backless kitchen chair, carving with a concentration that marked a true artisan. Only now there was one tiny difference.

Occasionally when I looked in, Mr. B. would glance up from his work, smile, and nod his head. Then, as if nothing had happened, he would turn back to his carving and continue his work.

One day, as fall approached, Danny and I finished cleaning up after the 5:45 AM Mass, and were heading out to Kaiser's Bakery for a piece of gingerbread before school. Father O'Phelan had taken his vestments off and we went over to tell him we were leaving.

"Wait a second, boys." Father said. "If you don't mind, I'd like you to help me for a moment."

It was unthinkable to say no to Father O'Phelan, so we followed him to the back of the church and over to his confessional.

"There are times when the hand of God reaches out and touches one in his distress," the sandy-haired senior assistant pastor told us as he picked up a hammer and nail from the pew. He must have put them there before Mass.

"At those times God allows not only the recipient of his healing to feel his hand, but those of us who stand in the shadows as well. Such a healing has taken place and, in thanksgiving for that, we are about to put a new crucifix in the confessional on the penitent's side."

Father picked up a small object that had been with the hammer and nail. It was a carved wooden crucifix that had been polished to a glasslike sheen. The cross was rough hewn but the body on it was smooth and showed the perfection sought by the carver.

"His hand..." Danny said as he pointed to the crucifix.

The right hand of the carved Savior seemed to have come free from its nail. Although the arm was still somewhat straight against the wood, the wrist and hand were turned toward us, reaching out, asking us to take it in our own hand.

I had never seen such a crucifix before—or since.

Danny held the flashlight and I held the crucifix until Father had the nail in just the right place. Then, taking the crucifix that he lovingly referred to as "the healing Savior," he hung it directly above the screen where the penitent knelt.

As we left the church, I started to ask Father O'Phelan if Mr. B. had been the one who had carved the crucifix, but Danny's poke stopped me cold. I didn't really need to ask, though. Without a single word, a lot of questions had been answered.

The confessionals are seldom used nowadays back in the old church. People confess "face to face," in reconciliation rooms. Perhaps the old confessional boxes are a thing of the past.

But I am sure if I ever want to go to confession when I visit St. Columbkille, I will ask to be heard in Father O'Phelan's old box, the one on the left side of the vestibule. Because I know—even if I can't see it in the darkness—that there is a hand held out out to me, beckoning me to follow him home.

Never Too Late

Every time I think of the 5:45 AM Mass at St. Columbkille, I think of Mr. Mulrennan who, like we altar boys, was a fixture at that unearthly hour's service.

I guess that Sister St. Patrick, the head honcho for the altar servers, felt that she had a divine mandate to put the name "Patrick" on the schedule for every 5:45 AM Mass. Beginning with David and moving down to us younger brothers, we had held the post for several years. It got to the point where we simply showed up, not even bothering to check the schedule except to see where else she had assigned us on the long list of weekly Masses.

We came to know all the "regulars" at that Mass: Pat and Tony, the two policemen who kept law and order in our neighborhood; Mr. Conneeley, who eventually married after almost six decades of bachelorhood; Mrs. O'Grady; and Mrs. O'Donnell, Seamus's mother. Mama often attended this Mass when she went early to someone's house to do their wash. And, of course, Mr. Mulrennan was there, half-kneeling and half-slumped over in the first pew, fingering his rosary beads and clearing his throat, day after day.

136

Mr. Mulrennan was a retired railroader who lived in a rented room in a boarding house a few doors from the church. He was a friend of Finneran, the janitor.

When communion time came, Mr. Mulrennan would hoist himself to a standing position and stomp to the communion rail with all the purpose shown by DeGaulle liberating Paris. As he waited, kneeling there at the rail, he would watch us as we proceeded down until we reached him.

After Communion he apparently thought it was no longer necessary to half-kneel and would slump back in the pew with his hand over his eyes and remain that way until the last prayer was said.

One day, as Danny snuffed out the candles and I cleaned up the cruets and put the missal ribbons in place for the seven o'clock Mass, Mr. Mulrennan stayed in his pew watching us do our tasks. He looked as if he were inspecting us to make sure we did everything right. Norbert Nowicki and Regan O'Farrell, who occasionally helped out at the Mass, were already taking their cassocks off in the boys' sacristy.

After we finished our jobs, Danny and I trotted off into the sacristy to take off our cassocks. When we had finished changing, we traipsed back through the sacristy to say "so long" to Father. We saw that Mr. Mulrennan had come into the sacristy, and was standing there talking quietly with Father Guilhooley, so we simply went out and headed off to school.

When the same thing happened the next day, we started to wonder what was going on. This time, though, Sister St. Patrick was part of the conversation between Father Guilhooley and Mr. Mulrennan. Our curiosity was piqued, to say the least.

It wasn't until about two weeks later that we learned the answer to our questions.

It was early May and Father Guilhooley was exercising his option to say the Mass of the Blessed Virgin which was his favorite Mass. So before we put on our cassocks, Danny and I set up the missal and lighted the candles on both the main altar and on the Blessed

Virgin altar, a pious practice that Father Guilhooley insisted on when he said that particular Mass. We knew that Father was already in the sacristy because Edward Guilhooley, Father's ancient Irish setter, was dozing in the door that opened into the sanctuary.

We hopped over Edward and nodded to Father as we went to the boys' sacristy to see if Regan or Norbert were there to help out.

"Huh?" Danny said when he pushed the door open.

Sister St. Patrick was standing in the sacristy along with Mr. Mulrennan, who was wearing a cassock and surplice and smiling sheepishly. Neither Regan nor Norbert was there.

"Mr. Mulrennan's going to serve with you boys today," Sister said matter-of-factly, "so you might have him serve at right acolyte."

Right acolyte was an easy position that required no particular skills other than to mount the altar steps at the consecration to lift the celebrant's chasuble. When there were only two servers, the one on the left side did the lifting while the one on the right rang the bell.

We could tell from Sister's expression that this was not the time to ask questions, so we simply did as we were told and got ready to serve Mass. Old Father Guilhooley had a funny sort of grin on his face, though, as we three servers lined up to go out on the altar. Even Edward did a double take as he moved out of the way to let us by.

Mr. Mulrennan did a credible job serving at right acolyte. He was a little slow-moving when he had to go up the three steps to lift the chasuble but did his job well, with just the right amount of piety.

When Mass was about over, Mr. Mulrennan fetched Father's biretta from the chair. We all genuflected and returned to the sacristy, then lined up for the traditional blessing from the celebrant.

Father Guilhooley blessed us and patted Edward like he always did because Edward would line up for the blessing with the rest of us. Then, putting his hands under his chasuble he grinned at the three servers standing there before him.

"So, Mulrennan," he said evenly, "how was it serving my Mass?"

The old man was beaming with pride and his eyes were moist as he stood there dressed in an altar boy's cassock and surplice.

"All my life I've wanted to serve at the altar, Father," Mr. Mulrennan said softly, "but I never had the chance. I thank you for lettin' me have me dream."

Father chuckled and turned back to unvest. Danny and I went back to the altar to put out the candles and fix the missal like always. Mr. Mulrennan followed us out and Danny handed him the candle snuffer so that he could help out.

When we had finished, we hung our cassocks up and Mr. Mulrennan went back out to the church. Sister St. Patrick was humming around the sacristy. She must have known that Danny and I were bursting with curiosity. She took pity on us, padded over to where we were standing, and told us to sit down on the bench.

"Mr. Mulrennan told Father that all his life he had wanted to be an altar boy," Sister St. Patrick said with a smile. "He was never able to be one when he was a child because he had to work on his father's farm in Galway. When Mr. Mulrennan came to America, he went to work on the railroad. Now that he no longer works and has the time to attend daily Mass, he found that the desire was still there. You may have noticed he's been carefully watching you boys to learn all about how to serve on the altar."

Danny grinned and nodded his head. I was still a little confused.

"So," she went on for my benefit, "when Mr. Mulrennan told Father about how he felt, Father said he could serve occasionally with you boys at the early Mass when there would be few people in the church."

It made sense. There was no law, after all, that said that an altar boy had to be a boy.

Mr. Mulrennan was never a regular server and he was never put on the Mass schedule. From time to time, however, he would glance at us as we prepared the altar to see if we needed an extra hand for the Mass. If we nodded, he would go on back to the sacristy to put on his cassock and surplice and take his place wherever he was needed. We never had to tell him what to do, when to ring the bells or when to fetch something. He had it all down pat—which, Danny said once, was better than I was when I was still half-asleep.

Now when I go to Mass, I watch the altar servers sometimes. Every so often I get the feeling that I would like to be a part of it again, holding the cruets for the celebrant, moving the missal, or even just snuffing out the candles after Mass.

But that's as far as I'll go. I don't have the sheer courage of the seventy-year-old man from Galway who braved the stares of the few people in the church to fulfill his desire to serve on the altar.

The All-of-Us Church

The vigil of Pentecost at St. Columbkille was formally devoted to cleaning the entire church from top to bottom. It was, as we often joked, the week the people at Murphy's Oil Soap lived for because of the copious amounts of that pungent liquid which we used to clean the church.

The students of St. Columbkille were part and parcel of the clean-up. Even the little tykes in the lower grades were put to work sorting hymn cards, paging through missals to ferret out and repair torn pages, and learning to pray the rosary as they worked.

Fourth, fifth, and sixth grades were assigned to scrub the pews and kneelers with the aforementioned Murphy's Oil Soap, while the seventh and eighth graders cleaned the statues, the floor, and the vast sanctuary of the church.

Clean-up work began right after the school Mass on Thursday morning and continued to the end of school on Friday. We had been told not to bring lunch on those two days, and we joked that the good Sisters would work us right through mealtime.

The truth was that Sister St. Chantal and Sister St. Vitus had pre-

141

pared a wonderful meal for us kids. Each kid, from the tiniest little guy to the biggest eighth grader, got a sandwich, an apple, two cookies, and a little sack of carrots or celery sticks.

Each year, four eighth graders—supposedly, it was a distinctive honor to be chosen—were assigned to clean the thirty-two million vigil candle cups encrusted with wax, soot, and the grunge that only years of flame could produce. Charlie, Victor, Regan, and I were the "lucky" crew for this year.

"Victor, you will be the water boy," said Sister St. Patrick as she prepared to demonstrate the method for cleaning the ruby, sapphire, and amber colored cups. "You'll need to keep changing the water because the water must be *hot*. Unless you use *hot* water you might as well not even *try* to clean these."

I was designated as the scraper. Sister gave me an ancient, totally dull kitchen paring knife with half a handle.

"Wrap a rag around the handle so you don't cut your hand," she admonished without a concerned glance at me, "and scrape *all* the wax from the glass *before* you put it in the water."

Charlie was the scrubber and wore rubber gloves because his hands would be in the hot water almost continuously.

Regan, the most finicky of us, was elected the polisher. It was his job to take a clean, dry cloth from the clean, dry cloth pile and wipe the little object until it sparkled with renewed gloss and was again a vigil light worthy of the name.

The job wasn't so bad once we got started, although my hand was quickly and permanently grooved by the broken knife handle. I soon perfected my technique: I would run a cut down the wax on the inside of the glass, slip the knife under an edge, and zip around the cup in a fluid motion. A practiced pop of the blade dislodged the wax on the bottom and another cup was ready for Charlie to scrub.

One advantage of this job was that we were put out on the stone steps of the church because of all the water that spilled and slopped over our work area. That meant we were able to sit in the warm sun and converse, something that the crews inside the church were forbidden to do.

We had been at our work for about an hour when Regan put another glass cup in the box and looked out onto Hardin Street.

"There goes another one!" he said to no one in particular.

"Another what?" Charlie asked.

Victor put a fresh bucket of steaming water down and picked up the one Charlie had been using.

"Another Sign of the Cross," Regan said. "That makes almost fifty since we've been out here." He meant, of course, the number of people who visibly and publicly made the Sign of the Cross when they passed the church.

We traded stories about the Sign of the Cross while we worked. Regan, who didn't need to closely watch his work like the rest of us did, kept unofficial score. As the morning wore on, he began counting men who tipped their hats, as well.

"Missed all those!" the redhead laughed when a streetcar passed on the tracks in front of the church. "I bet I would have to add fifty if I could've seen all of 'em!"

Bloke, Brian, and some of our other cronies joined us out in front of the church at lunchtime. Sister said we could gather where we wanted and the steps of the huge church seemed to be a logical place. A half-dozen girls came out and sat on the trimmed grass that framed either side of the front of the church and joined in our conversation.

"Here comes the food!" Shiela McHale called just as the first peal of the Angelus sounded from the tower.

Finneran, who had been pulling his homemade cart with the sandwiches and other goodies in it stopped dead in his tracks and pulled off his cap.

"The Angel of the Lord declared unto Mary!" Finneran called out in his heavy brogue.

"And she conceived of the Holy Ghost!" we answered back, looking up at the tower.

The ground we sat on actually shook when the massive Queen

of Peace bell joined her three smaller companions at the end of the salutation to the Mother of God. Finneran resumed distributing lunches as Regan excitedly told us exactly how many persons along Hardin Street stopped and stood in prayer during the Angelus.

"Even Reverend Tracy stopped and prayed!" Regan beamed.

That was nothing new to us. The Presbyterian minister was never one to quibble about the origin of a prayer, and he took advantage of every opportunity he had to praise God.

As I listened to Regan, I began to realize that I was surrounded by people who were unafraid to show their faith in God. From old men to young boys and girls; ladies like Mama who carried their work dresses in paper sacks or grande dames like Mrs. Bennett who wore furs even in the summer; from nuns and priests to little, plump ministers and towering Lutheran pastors; even Rabbi Hirsch and the Sapersteins—all had a way of showing respect when they passed St. Columbkille.

We showed the same respect when we passed by or entered the places of worship of other denominations. We would lower our voices and pull off our caps when we went by Reverend Tracy's little church, on our way to pick up his son, Denis, or drop off an extra newspaper.

Sometimes, after playing ball or attending a Boy Scout meeting, several of us would kneel in the cool sanctuary of St. James Lutheran church beside our buddy, Jim Hoch, whose grandfather was the pastor there. We would silently pray for a few minutes, each in our own words, reflecting our own beliefs.

The first time I went to Temple Beth Israel, it felt strange to cover my head in a church. After that, when I would visit the temple on occasion, I would automatically reach for a yarmulke when the man held one out. And I will always remember the warmth of the little squeeze on the shoulders Rabbi Hirsch would give us "goyim" as he draped a prayer shawl over our shoulders.

"Look at these sparkle!" Regan said, not without some personal satisfaction, as he finished filling another box with the glass cups.

"I bet I carried more water than they have in Lake Erie!" Victor said, rubbing his arm. His pants were soaked from water that had spilled over the top of the bucket, and he had long ago taken off his shoes and socks to keep them from getting them wet as well.

The pile of wax shards on the canvas tarp in front of me was almost a foot high. Charlie grinned from ear to ear as he pulled off his rubber gloves to show us his fingers, wrinkled like prunes from being in water all day.

We were about three-fourths done, Sister St. Patrick told us at the end of the day. Tomorrow we would finish up and, by noon, she expected the church to be back to normal and ready for another year of use.

As usual, Sister was right to the second. By noon Regan had polished the last glass and we watched as Brian O'Neill and Arthur Wunderlich carted the final box of vigil lamps back into the church. Charlie dumped the last bucket of water into the storm drain and went off to put the buckets away. I watched Finneran load my wax into a large trash bag and rubbed my sore hands to get the little film of wax off them. Victor mopped around the stairs to make sure the area was safe to walk on.

The rest of the students came out of the church as they finished their tasks, and we all milled around outside waiting for the signal to go back to school. After a while Sister St. Patrick and Sister St. Kermit came out the door of the church and smiled. Monsignor and the two assistant priests followed them out and grinned as well.

Without any words, we were led, eighth graders first, into the newly cleaned church. I looked around in awe as I dipped my fingers into the cleaned, crystal-clear holy water font. The windows, always impressive but now more so than usual, let shimmering jewels of color float in the hallowed air of the sanctuary. The brass and gold fixtures, polished by the sixth grade, blazed with a fire I had never noticed before.

The polished wood of the vast pews shone from the glow of Murphy's soap. Our mottled marble floor was like a mirror and I almost hesitated to walk on it. When I did, it was with a light step, as if I were walking on air.

Best of all, from every nook and cranny, from every side, angle, and alcove, tiny pinpoints of light flickered from the vigil candle cups that Victor, Charlie, Regan and I had scraped, washed, and polished until our fingers were raw.

"Like the hallways of heaven!" Regan exclaimed dramatically.

We didn't laugh at him, though. He was right. I put my arm around my friend's shoulder and basked in the satisfaction of knowing that we had been a part of all this.

After the 5:45 AM Mass the next morning, I told Father O'Phelan how we felt during our clean-up the day before. I told him about watching people tip their hats and make the Sign of the Cross when they passed by the church. I also told about how we acted in the other churches and synagogues of our neighborhood, and how Ritchie, Noam, Denis, and Jim felt as much a part of St. Columbkille as we felt part of their places of worship.

"It's called *ekklesia*, Sean-o," the priest grinned, "and it's the Greek word we use for 'church.'"

I nodded, anxious to agree.

"Like St. Columbkille is a...a...*ekklesia!*" I said, not really understanding what he was getting at.

"No," Father said, kindly, "like *us. We* are *ekklesia*. Church is *who*, Sean-o, not what. *We* are church—you and me, Sister, Victor," he winked at my English friend, "Ritchie, Denis, Noam, and Jim."

I thought about this for a moment. I remembered the feeling I had when I was with my friends, the close friendship we shared regardless of race, religion, or nationality.

We were *ekklesia* and always will be—who, and not what.

"Praise Him, All Creatures..."

I don't know when I first heard the word "ecumenism," but I am certain I was well into adulthood. Back in the dark ages of the 1940s and 50s Catholics were expected to refrain from involvement with people of other faiths, and so we kept pretty much to ourselves.

St. Columbkille, though, was not bound by the traditional aloofness we saw in many other parishes. The parish was located in the heart of the inner city where there seemed to be a church on every block. St. James Lutheran, for example, was only a block away and we knew almost everyone who attended that church. Pastor Hoch, a German pastor of the old school, was best friends with our own founding pastor, Father Guilhooley.

If we walked a block in the other direction we stood on the steps of Temple Beth Israel, with its carved doors and seven-branched candlestick above them. Ritchie Saperstein went here with his family so we reasoned that it must be a fine place. Rabbi Hirsch got his daily newspaper from my brother Danny on Patrick's Corner and knew us all by name.

The smallest church was the Presbyterian church, which was down the street from St. James. It was a tiny wooden structure that seated about one hundred people—if they didn't mind brushing up against each other in the pews. Danny had made friends with Denis Tracy whose father was pastor of this congregation. The fact that he was Presbyterian and Irish did not sit too well with Mama at first, but Denis was quick to win her over. After a while, Mama even became friends with Reverend and Mrs. Tracy.

Still, with all our proximity and friendliness, the people in each of these different churches really did not mix with one another. It was understood that, while one could be friends with a person of a different faith, taking part in his or her worship service was frowned upon and something one just did not do.

Because of the friendship between Danny and Denis, we spent a good deal of our time over at the Tracy house, which was attached to the little church.

Denis had certain chores to do over at the church such as straightening the hymnbooks and the Bibles in the pews and sweeping the smooth wooden floor before services. And so many times, on our way to the swimming hole or to the lagoon for ice skating, Danny and Ritchie and Bloke and I would hurry into the "Presbyterian" to help Denis get his work done faster and move us all along the road to doing the more important things in life. We never minded helping out and considered it an act of kindness to a friend.

At other times we would arrive to fetch Denis for something or other on a Sunday just as the morning service was ending. We stood outside the church and listened to Reverend Tracy's voice as he led the congregation in prayer or instructed them in the ways of God. Still, taking part in a service was something one just did not do, so we stood out of the way and made sure we weren't too loud when we caught ourselves saying the Lord's Prayer with the rest of the congregation.

This separation was all well and good—until Danny and I received an invitation in the mail requesting "the honor of your presence at 11:00 AM next Sunday for the Confirmation in the Faith of Denis Martin Tracy."

"I didn't even know they *had* confirmation!" Danny exclaimed when he showed me the invitation.

"Will our bishop be there to do it?" I asked innocently, earning a glare from my brother.

"What are we gonna tell him?" I said, convinced that we would never be allowed to attend a Presbyterian service unless we were forced in at gunpoint.

Danny shook his head.

"Sheesh!" he muttered in his patented sigh of frustration.

I thought it over and made a brilliant suggestion.

"Maybe we can stand outside like we do on Sundays. That way we can be there but not inside."

I thought some more.

"Unless it rains...."

Mama was more helpful but she did not solve the problem.

"I think what you need to do is show the invitation to Monsignor."

I looked at Danny and he looked at me.

"Maybe he can tell us we have to serve the eleven o'clock Mass that day!" I said, thinking that an obligation of that magnitude would be sufficient an excuse to allow us to extend our regrets.

We walked to the rectory with the invitation.

"I really would like to go, Sean-o," Danny muttered as we trudged along, "'cause Din is my best friend. He's your friend, too."

I agreed. In spite of the fact that we would be sure to hear "no" when we asked Monsignor about attending, I too really wanted to be there for Denis' ceremony and to rejoice with him and his family.

"We could go to the little party afterwards. They don't pray at that!" Danny said, desperately forming a plan for compromise.

It wouldn't be the same, I felt. If you were going to the party you should at least be there for the service. It was kind of like going to the wake and missing the funeral.

Monsignor was walking up and down the stone walk in the garden, reading from his breviary. He glanced up as he saw us approaching. I guess the serious expression on our faces told him that we were there on weighty matters because he closed the book and stood waiting for us to tell him our problem.

Danny showed Monsignor the invitation and explained our predicament. It wasn't like we would be praying, Danny told him, just standing or sitting in the church as an act of support for our friend.

"We can think of other stuff!" I suggested brilliantly, trying to provide an alternative for being there.

Monsignor harrumphed and frowned at me.

"Why would you not be praying for your best friend?" the prelate asked bluntly.

"Huh?" Danny stammered.

"It's a wonderful thing that Denis is being confirmed, isn't it? He's a fine, fine lad. I see him often when he comes here with you for basketball. He sits in the pew on Saturday waiting for you boys when you come for confession. Why would you not pray for him? I'm sure he prays for you!"

I had no doubt that Din prayed for us. He was that kind of kid.

"But we're not supposed to go to non-Catholic services," Danny spouted.

We got another "harrumph!"

"Wear your best clothes so the Presbyterians can see we Catholics know how to show respect in church!" Monsignor said.

That was it? No argument? No conditions?

Monsignor opened his breviary to where he had left off, and began walking away.

Danny and I were ecstatic when we arrived home. Mama was relieved to hear that we could go to the confirmation, and she promised to bake two pans of scones to contribute to the festivities after the ceremony.

The Presbyterian service before the confirmation was quite different from our Catholic Mass. There were several hymns that we did not know and the sermon was the main part of the celebration.

Din and four other kids—three boys and one girl—were asked to come forward and profess their devotion to the faith and to serving God. I felt immensely proud that I was there, witnessing our friend stand before his father and put his hands into the Reverend's.

As the ceremony drew to a close I looked around the church. I was astounded to see the hulking figure of Monsignor Hanratty at the end of the last pew. Father O'Phelan sat next to him, and their stark black suits made them stand out among the more festive frocks of the regular worshippers.

"We will end this service by singing the 'Old Hundredth,'" Reverend Tracy said, opening his hymn book.

I didn't know that song and I was glad that the lady sitting next to me handed me a hymn book for Danny and me to share.

The little organ sounded and we all stood up.

"Praise God from whom all blessings flow! Praise him all creatures here below!"

I felt goosebumps creep up my arms as the tiny congregation thundered out the words with meaning and devotion.

"Praise him above, ye heavenly host!"

I knew that in spite of ritual, in spite of tradition, in spite of history, we were all there for the very same purpose.

"Praise Father, Son, and Holy Ghost!"

I could hear the powerful bass voice of Monsignor as he joined the Presbyterians in song. I felt as if our friendship with Din and his parents was now confirmed and sealed, stamped with the approval of the highest power. I hoped and prayed our friend would be blessed on this special day.

Some years later, our group of friends would gather for the ordination of Reverend Denis Martin Tracy. Only by that time it would be common to participate in the services of those in other faiths.

Still later, when Din's dad, the Reverend Martin Tracy, was laid to rest, the church was packed to the seams with people even gathered outside as Denis preached the most powerful sermon of his life. His words were heard by almost a thousand people, many—most—from places other than the Hardin Street Presbyterian Church.

By that time, I knew what "ecumenism" meant. And I had come to realize that it was something I had been practicing for all my life.

A Great *Ekklesia*

Monsignor Hanratty always looked the other way when Father O'Phelan "did his own thing." And, I suppose, Monsignor may have been chided a bit by his fellow pastors for his unofficial ecumenism in the days before ecumenism was an acceptable word.

But I'm getting ahead of myself.

Back in 1950, Father O'Phelan was preparing for the annual Youth Retreat which was held over a weekend for all high school students from the parish. The retreat was held just at the end of the football season and just before the basketball season so that none of the students would have a good excuse for missing it. My brothers and I wouldn't have missed it for the world, though. It was a time for business—God's business, to be sure. But it was also a fun time because we spent the entire weekend, from Friday evening until Sunday vespers, camping out in the gym, taking part in activities in the social hall, and generally enjoying each other's company.

During the week before the retreat, Danny had arranged for us to use the gym one evening to play basketball. Finneran left the place unlocked for us and Danny, Kevin, and I gathered up Bloke,

Brian O'Neill, Mike Polanski, and Joey Stolarski for an evening of sport. On the way, Danny suggested asking Denis Tracy, Ritchie and Noam Saperstein, and Jim Hoch to come along. The more of us there were, the more fun we could have.

When we all arrived at the gym, Father O'Phelan was standing outside on the stairs talking with Finneran. Father had been hanging some posters for the retreat on the walls of the gym, and we stopped to admire them.

Ritchie, Noam, Denis, and Jim asked about the posters, and Danny explained a bit about the retreat.

"Sounds like it's a great time," Denis said, as we went out on the court to play our game.

After we finished playing and had showered, we roamed out into the gym to find Father O'Phelan looking over the posters. Danny walked over to a corner of the gym and announced that he was "reserving" his spot for the retreat.

"I've had this spot for two years, Father, and I mean to keep it!" he said, grinning at the friendly priest.

Denis and Ritchie were still curious about the retreat, and they peppered Father with questions about it. The flustered priest tried his best to answer them.

"Well, boys," Father finally said, "why don't you ask your parents if you can make the retreat with your friends this year?"

Jim Hoch smiled.

"My grandfather is best friends with old Father Guilhooley," he said, "I bet I could come if I ask."

Ritchie, who had made his bar mitzvah in our social hall when the temple was being repaired after a fire, said he felt like he and Noam actually belonged to St. Columbkille anyway. Denis was as much a part of our lives as anyone so we knew that his father would allow him to come.

We didn't realize then that Father O'Phelan was a bit out of his league by inviting the others, and that he had taken on a bit more than he might be able to chew.

Permission to attend the retreat was readily granted by the parents and pastors involved. But that wasn't the problem. The difficulty arose because some of the parishioners raised their eyebrows when they found out that some non-Catholic kids were going to make a Catholic retreat with the rest of us.

Fortunately, we kids didn't hear any of the comments. And so we made our retreat along with our friends, who participated in all the events and enjoyed the time as much as we did. Father O'Phelan conducted a good retreat. He included Denis, Ritchie, Noam, and Jim in our discussions without letting on that there was a subtle movement afoot to eliminate this type of openness from any future activities at St. Columbkille Church.

At the close of the retreat, which was held at Sunday Vespers, we gathered in the front of the packed church for the chanting of the Office. All of us were filled with renewed enthusiasm after our retreat. We took up almost six pews on either side, the boys on the epistle side and the girls on the gospel side. Jim Hoch was on my left and Noam Saperstein was on my right.

After the chanting of Vespers, Monsignor Hanratty began the solemn Benediction. Monsignor exposed the Blessed Sacrament and we sang *Tantum Ergo* while it was incensed. Then, uncharacteristically, he trotted over to the side of the altar and sat down. Father O'Phelan mounted the high pulpit and looked out over the congregation.

"I welcome you all to God's house!" he called out loudly.

The congregation shifted a bit, not knowing what was going on.

"I said," he exclaimed, louder than before, "to God's house...*not* to church."

Now we too were shifting around.

"We have come to think of the word 'church' as meaning a place of worship, a building. As St. Columbkille," he paused, "or as Saint James Lutheran or Hardin Street Presbyterian or Temple Beth Israel."

He looked around and softened his tone.

"When I was a young seminarian I had to study the Scriptures in

Greek," he said. "In so doing that I learned that the word *ekklesia*—used often in Acts and in the epistles, the word which we translate as 'church'—meant something far different than I had suspected. When I learned what I am about to tell you, it changed my life. And, I hope and pray, it may even change your lives if you'll take but a moment to listen."

He spoke frankly, almost academically.

"Instead of a building or a place, the writer of the Acts meant something quite specific and unique with the word *ekklesia*. He used the word to mean a gathering together of the people of God."

Father O'Phelan paused and cleared his throat. He only did that when he was nervous so we knew that he was trying to deliver a very important message.

"This weekend," he said, now looking at the students, "we have had a chance to experience what church—*ekklesia*—is really all about. We have been blessed with having not one, but four young people of other faiths take part in our annual youth retreat. They came with the blessing of their parents and the blessing of their own pastors. They came freely, not to be changed into Catholics but to be changed into more powerful witnesses for God."

A few people cleared their throats. The shifting around was more evident; some of the people there knew they were being told that they had been wrong in their criticism.

"This weekend, our young people gathered together as the people of God. We lighted our candles together and sang our psalms as one, not as Catholics or Protestants or as Jews. We held hands in a circle and we asked God to bless us, our parents, and our lives."

He looked over at us.

"We came together not as the people of St. Columbkille or Saint James Lutheran or Hardin Street Presbyterian or Temple Beth Israel," he said in a whisper, looking at us with affection, "but as the people of God."

"I know you're not prepared, but I wonder if any of you young visitors would like to say anything about what you might have gained from this weekend?"

There was a long silence. Then Ritchie Saperstein raised his hand and stood up.

"I'm Richard Saperstein," he said softly. "I learned that even my sports and my schoolwork give God glory when I do them like I'm supposed to and for the right reasons."

Father smiled and nodded. Then Jim Hoch raised his hand and stood up.

"I'm Jim Hoch from Saint James. I learned that since we have to live together we'd best get to know each other as friends. I made a whole bunch of new friends this weekend!" (Jim was the most popular boy at the retreat because of his easygoing personality and good humor.)

Next, Denis stood up. He was a shy boy and spoke softly. "I'm Denis Tracy. My dad's the minister over at Hardin Street Presbyterian. I've always had a lot of friends from St. Columbkille. Now I know just how much I really love 'em all...and Jim and Ritchie and Noam, too."

Father pointed to Noam Saperstein who was waving his hand in the air. Noam was younger than the rest of us and he stood up a bit self-consciously.

"My name is Noam Saperstein," the boy said. "I just feel good about the whole weekend. I'm gonna ask our Rabbi if we can't have something like this at Beth Israel! I never knew how good it feels to share with other kids my own age."

Father leaned out over the pulpit. Monsignor sat smugly, trying not to smile too much.

"What I mean to say, good people," Father said gently, "is that right now we are enjoying the fullness of God's message to us. We are *ekklesia* at this moment. We are 'church' in the only sense intended by that word. Right now we are in a building of worship called St. Columbkille. In a few minutes we will be out and going about our lives. But we will still be 'church' wherever we are because we cannot limit our *ekklesia* to a building or to a particular denomination."

He asked Jim, Denis, Ritchie, and Noam to stand up again.

"I wish to thank you boys for bringing us this most meaningful message and I am certain we shall all remember your contribution to this exciting weekend."

Uncharacteristically for the time, a faint smattering of applause started somewhere back in the congregation and then spread until it sounded like thunder. Monsignor looked around and then applauded, himself.

We finished Benediction, then chanted Compline together. Then, we went back to the school and gathered our stuff from the gym. From there we each went back to our own homes, our own worlds, which had been greatly enriched because of Father O'Phelan.

After that, there was no more criticism when non-Catholics were invited to participate in various events. The inclusion of friends became a regular part of the yearly retreat, and we felt free to invite others along.

The miracles of modern life—television, two cars in every garage, shopping malls, and the like—have taken us out of our provincialism and thrust us into a whirlwind where "church" has become a place again, instead of a principle of living.

But, perhaps *ekklesia* is not all gone. Perhaps there are priests like Father O'Phelan who stand before us and tell us who we are again.

"Wake up!" I want those priests to say, "And look around you! Come out of the world of "you" and into the world of "us"! We are *ekklesia*—the gathering of the people of God, so let's act like it!"

And perhaps we may just listen to him and stand a bit taller as we leave our house of worship, a bit better off than when we entered.

Ritchie Saperstein's First Confession

I don't think anything could have matched the sweet aroma of the steaming hot dog that day, or the tingling warmth on my fingertips as I held the tissue-wrapped bun.

I smeared a good-sized gob of yellow mustard on the hot dog, and the pungent smell of that delectable condiment made my eyes smart as I took my first bite. I had waited all day long for this moment!

But no sooner had I savored that first morsel when Bloke came by, hollering the words that ruined the rest of my day.

"Sean-o! It's Friday!!!"

I had eaten meat on Friday.

Without any doubt, I was now doomed to the lowest level of hell.

My face suddenly turned crimson. I looked down at the hot dog and knew I would have to throw it away. Worse, I would have to wait until the next day to confess this sin and be saved from the fires of damnation.

I hurried over to Patrick's Corner. Ritchie Saperstein and Victor

Doyle were there because they liked to hang around Danny and me when the weather was nice. I related my tale of woe to the boys, and Danny berated me for being so dumb as to have forgotten what day of the week it was.

While this was going on, Ritchie was earnestly listening to Victor explain what I had done, and how I could be forgiven for this dastardly deed and saved from eternal torment.

"You mean that confession stuff will get you back in good with God?" Ritchie asked.

He had known about confession. Many Saturdays when he was on his way to or from temple, we would be on our way to confession, and we would all stop to talk before we each went on our way. Before some of the major feasts Ritchie would sit in one of the pews in St. Columbkille, waiting for us finish our holiday confessions and get back to whatever game we had been playing.

"Sean-o will go to confession tomorrow and tell Father O'Phelan that he ate meat on Friday, and Father will tell him that he's a lout and not to do it again," Victor was saying. "Then Sean-o will have to say some prayers and he's all forgiven."

It was a simplistic way of describing the sacrament, but to our way of thinking it pretty well covered what confession did for the soul.

"What if Father thinks Sean-o is going to eat another hot dog?"

It was a fair question, and Ritchie knew me well enough to expect a scam.

"Then Sean-o will have to convince him that he has a firm purpose of amendment," Victor said.

Bloke explained to Ritchie that that meant I had to be pretty sorry for eating the hot dog and promise not to do it again unless I forgot (which was not likely with my brother and my friends around).

"How 'bout if you rob a bank?" Ritchie was getting to the heart of confession.

"Father makes you give the money back and you have to promise not to rob a bank again," Bloke said matter-of-factly.

The conversation was making me feel a bit better. I had said an act of contrition, which would hold me over until confession time on Saturday—or so I hoped. I was truly sorry—sorry that I had taken a bite out of the hot dog and sorry that I had to throw the rest away, uneaten. That was the real thing about confession: you had to be sorry, and not just because you got caught.

The theology of not eating meat on Friday and the spiritual renewal we felt each time we received the sacrament did not enter into our conversation.

"That's real neat," Ritchie said as he settled back against the barber shop window to watch us work and to think about the cleverness of Catholic living.

We worked until it was almost twilight, then I packed up my shoeshine box while Danny went into the Shamrock Pub with the two or three newspapers he had left. He could always get rid of the last few in there.

"I sure wish Jews had something like that for when they have something on their mind," Ritchie said as we all walked home.

"Well, Jesus invented confession and he was a Jew," Victor said, sincerely.

The next day was Saturday. Confessions were heard from three until six every Saturday and the church was always crowded. Danny and I liked to go early, around three o'clock, so we could get in and out without having to wait forever in Father O'Phelan's line.

We were in luck. The church had not yet begun to fill and Father O'Phelan waved as he headed for his confessional. Danny brushed me aside and hurried to the penitent's door. Bloke, Victor, and Charlie Carroll had come in and were crowding together in a pew when Danny came out.

As he went up to the communion rail to say his penance, I went in to the box and confessed the heinous deed of having taken a bite out of a hot dog on the day before.

"Why only a bite, Sean-o?" Father asked with some puzzlement in his voice.

"Well, Bloke hollered that it was Friday, so I tossed the rest in the trash."

Father laughed and gently told me that I was not doomed to the fires of hell. He said that my slip-up was human error, not something done to offend a loving God.

I was still miffed that I could have been so dumb as to eat a hot dog on Friday, so I felt a bit better when he gave me five Our Fathers and five Hail Marys to make up for my misdeed. I said an act of contrition while Father murmured the words of absolution. Then, feeling like a washed-clean Christian, I got up and opened the door of the confessional.

As I stepped out, someone rushed by me into the confessional and pulled the door shut. I turned to see who it was but my eyes hadn't adjusted to the sudden light after having knelt in the dark confessional.

"Ssssssssss!!" Bloke and Victor were waving at me wildly.

"Ritchie's in the confessional!" they hissed when I came up to them.

"What?" I gasped.

They told me that Bloke was just about to get up when he saw me come out of the confessional.

"Then Ritchie just pushed past Bloke and went in there, for corn sakes!"

A Jew in our confessional?

Bloke and Victor moaned audibly, blaming themselves for not noticing Ritchie in the semi-darkness of the church. I self-righteously remained aloof because I had been in the confessional and hadn't seen Ritchie in the first place.

Danny had finished saying his penance and had come back to the pew. He dragged me outside by the arm so that I could tell him what all the commotion was about.

"Cor!" he gasped when I told him that our Jewish friend was in the confessional.

I was about to go back inside to say my penance when the side door opened and Ritchie stepped out into the afternoon sunlight. Charlie Carroll and Victor were with him. The smile on his face was genuine and radiant.

"Where's Bloke?" Danny asked.

"Tellin' his sins," Charlie Carroll supplied.

"Man! What did you do *that* for, Ritchie?" I faced the problem directly.

"When I heard you guys talk about being forgiven yesterday, I got to thinking...well, I've got some stuff that needs forgiving, too."

Ritchie said that there were things in his life that had been bothering him. He told us that on Yom Kippur, the Jewish Day of Atonement, he always prayed for forgiveness and promised to live better during the coming year.

"But it ain't always easy to do," he said. We nodded our heads in agreement. "And Yom Kippur is just once a year."

He had a point.

"So, I thought I'd give your confession stuff a crack!"

"Did Father kill you for comin' into a confessional?" Victor asked.

Ritchie shook his head.

"I guess he knew I wasn't Catholic, but he listened to me and gave me some hints about how to be better."

That sounded like Father O'Phelan.

"Then he told me to say some prayers and to tell God I'm really sorry for my sins."

We could see that our friend was beaming in the knowledge of God's forgiveness, that he had truly felt the loving hand of the Lord.

Later on, Danny got up the gumption to ask Father O'Phelan if he knew that he had heard the confession of a non-Catholic.

"You mean when Ritchie came in to tell me about his faults? Naturally I knew it was Ritchie. I've known him and Noam since they were just little guys."

"But..." Danny looked a bit startled.

"You boys talk to Rabbi Hirsch. If one of you had a problem and a priest was not around, would you hesitate to go to him and ask his advice?"

We shook our heads. Rabbi Hirsch was respected by just about everyone for his knowledge and for his willingness to listen.

"You, Daniel. You're best friends with Denis Tracy; his father is a Presbyterian minister. How many times have you gone to Reverend Tracy when you needed help with something personal?"

Danny grinned. It was no secret that Danny had often sat with the Reverend in the quiet of the tiny Presbyterian church when he felt bothered or alone. I had done so myself, sometimes sharing things with Reverend Tracy that I couldn't even tell Danny.

Father O'Phelan went on. "Did Jesus come for only a few? He came for us all and his Father made us all. Ritchie is as much mine as you all are, just as you all belong to Rabbi Hirsch and to Reverend Tracy. God is not particular about who he forgives!"

We grinned in appreciation.

"I did tell Ritchie it might be better if he just comes to the rectory and asks for me!" Father O'Phelan said with a smile. "I imagine his running into the confessional made some hubbub in the pews!"

We nodded in agreement. Danny walked over to the priest and gave him a quick hug.

We never kidded Ritchie about his first confession, although we might have if we hadn't understood the depth of his need and the reason for his action.

Ritchie's experience opened up new doors for us, too. From then on, when Ritchie confided in one of us, we didn't hesitate to recommend a trip to the rectory. And when he did make that trip he invariably returned with a lighter step and an infectious grin.

"What penance did Father give you, Ritchie?" we sometimes kidded.

"Psalm 23," Ritchie might answer. Or, "Psalm 121; always the Psalms!"

And why not?

"Why Is This Night Different from All Other Nights?"

No one could ever accuse Father O'Phelan of being anything other than ultra-orthodox when it came to the teachings of the Roman Catholic Church. His devotion to the *Magisterium Ecclesiae* was legend, and he was forever studying the various encyclicals and documents from the Vatican, trying to be more informed and a better priest for his flock.

Still, in spite of being more Catholic than the Pope, Father was also among the most open-minded of men. His friendships encompassed people of virtually every nationality, religion, and race and most were surprised when they found out he usually knew more about their cultures than they themselves did.

It was the spring of 1950, when I was a freshman at Holy Redeemer High School. Father O'Phelan had scheduled an after school meeting for the senior altar boys to prepare for the upcoming Holy Week services. Kevin and Danny were there, along with a bunch of regulars. Since we were going to use the gym to play basketball after the meeting, our friends Ritchie Saperstein and Denis Tracy were there, too.

Father was telling us about Holy Thursday, explaining how it evolved from the Passover.

"You celebrate Passover in your family, don't you Ritchie?" Father asked, turning to our friend.

"Sure, Father," Ritchie grinned, "every year. It starts this weekend, in fact, on Friday night."

Father asked Ritchie to explain what went on during the Seder, the Passover supper, and we listened to him with interest.

"We have a Lord's Supper," Denis told us, "and it sounds a little bit like that."

"It is, Denis," Father O'Phelan said. "Jesus used the sacred feast of Passover to institute the Eucharist which we now call communion. It was the first Mass for us Catholics."

At the end of our meeting, we stayed on to play basketball. Father O'Phelan disappeared and we didn't see him again that day.

The next day, however, Danny and I were on our way home after selling newspapers and shining shoes on Patrick's Corner when Ritchie hurried after us, yelling to wait up.

Breathlessly, he told us that Father O'Phelan had visited his father and mother after our meeting and had arranged for all of the altar servers to share the Passover meal with the Saperstein family on Friday night.

"Your ma's gonna cook for the whole mess of us?" Danny asked in awe.

"No big thing," Ritchie grinned, "but you have to bring your own plates because we don't have enough for you goyim to eat from!"

I remembered that the Sapersteins always pulled out a special set of dishes when I ate with them because their religion said that they couldn't let non-Jews use their tableware. I didn't understand why but it never really bothered me. We Catholics had some pretty strange practices too, I thought.

On the night of the Seder meal, Kevin, Danny, and I stopped at Bloke's to pick him up. We met Regan O'Farrell along the way, and saw Reverend Tracy and Denis going inside the Sapersteins' building just as we reached the corner. It looked like it was going to be a good crowd. It also looked kind of strange because we were all carrying plates and had silverware in our pockets!

We went up the three flights of stairs to the apartment. When we got there, I noticed dark streaks over the door which I hadn't seen before. I touched the mezuzah on the door frame then put my fingers to my lips the way Ritchie had shown me when I was at his place on other occasions.

Father O'Phelan was already there as we entered the bustling apartment. It was getting dark outside, and the only light in the place came from the candles burning on the tables. From my friendship with Ritchie, I knew that the Jews were not allowed to work anything mechanical, including light switches or stoves, after sun set on the evening of the Sabbath.

Ritchie's grandfather and father came over to welcome us.

"Such a nice thing, all of you together!" the old man said, kissing each of us on the cheek as we settled in.

We put our plates on the table and were told where to stand. Ritchie moved in back of us, handing each of us a thin prayer shawl to put on our shoulders and a yarmulke for our heads.

"I borrowed these from temple," Ritchie said, and grinned as we readied for the Passover meal.

Ritchie's father took his place at the head of the crowded table.

"Before we begin our Seder," he said, "did you notice the blood over the doorway?" Mr. Saperstein looked around at us bathed in the light of the menorah which was placed in the center of the table,

We nodded. Then he told us how the Israelites marked their doors with the blood of the lamb to identify them to God's avenging angel prior to the exodus from Egypt.

"The angel would pass over the homes so marked," he said, "which is why we call this day the Passover."

Danny noticed that there were no chairs at the table. "Do we sit down to eat?" he asked.

Ritchie handed his father a long wooden rod to hold.

"We will eat while standing, with our shawls on our shoulders and as I hold out my staff," Mr. Saperstein said, "because, like the ancient Israelites, we are preparing for our journey."

He looked around and asked if we had any more questions before the Passover started. We didn't, so he nodded to Ritchie's brother Noam, who was the youngest male in the household.

The dark-eyed twelve year old cleared his throat and read from a little piece of paper.

"Father," he asked in a soft voice, "why is this night different from all other nights?"

"Because, my son," Mr. Saperstein answered, looking at all of us, "on this night God delivered his people from bondage."

We ate while standing, sharing the stiff, dry matzo, dipping the bitter herb into the little bowls of salted water, passing the goblet of sweet wine from hand to hand. Mr. Saperstein explained the significance of each kind of food and the reason why various questions were asked as the meal progressed.

I could almost feel the brush of the angel's wings as I stood there, surrounded by God's people—*ekklesia*—remembering God's mercy with a ritual that was older than most of the buildings or nations on the face of the earth. Here, at one table, stood a Jewish family, a Catholic priest and five altar boys, and a Presbyterian minister and his son; different faiths but a common background.

After the meal, we rinsed our plates in a special pan of water. As I handed my shawl to Ritchie, I grinned. I could see he was proud to have been able to share the Seder meal with his friends.

"Shalom, Sean-o!" he said as he took the shawl and yarmulke.

"Shalom, Ritchie!" I smiled back.

"You look pretty neat in your beanie, Din!" said Danny, grinning as he put his arm around Denis. "Next thing we know you'll want to wear one at the Presbyterian!"

"Father O'Phelan," said Grandpa Saperstein, "would you and Reverend Tracy say a blessing, too? It would not seem right to have you with us and not ask your blessing on us, as well."

Father looked around and smiled.

"Of course, Mr. Saperstein," he said.

We altar boys knelt down like we usually did. Reverend Tracy took off his hat and stood next to Father O'Phelan.

Father O'Phelan looked at the varied flock around him and lifted his eyes upward.

"There is only one blessing for a gathering such as this," he said, *"Sh'ma yisrael, adonai elohenu, adonai echad!"*

The grandfather's eyes beamed as he heard the priest pray in flawless Hebrew.

"Amen!" Reverend Tracy said.

"What does that mean?" Regan O'Farrell hissed.

"It means, Regan," Reverend Tracy said, putting on his hat, "'Hear, O Israel, the Lord our God, the Lord is one!'"

It was a fitting way, indeed, to end this unique gathering, and a blessing that I have remembered all my life.

When we were back at home that evening, we told Mama and our other brothers about our Seder at the Sapersteins. David said he wished he had gone along. Mama said that it sounded very nice and that she was glad we didn't break the plates.

Less than a week later I stood in the sanctuary of St. Columbkille Church during the Holy Thursday evening Mass. Kevin was holding the thurible, watching intently as the Mass progressed after the washing of the feet. Danny and Bloke stood over by the credence table and Regan O'Farrell was close by Monsignor Hanratty's elbow as he prepared for the consecration. Father O'Phelan and Father O'Toole were in their places on the altar listening to Monsignor's slow, cadenced Latin prayers.

For a moment, I felt as if I was again standing at the Sapersteins' table, watching my brothers and friends as the light of the menorah danced on their features, as we prepared for a journey and waited for the angel to pass us by.

As we approached the consecration I carried the incense bowl over to where Kevin stood so that Father O'Phelan could place the sweet incense onto the coals in Kev's thurible. Father might have been thinking about the Passover, too, and its ties to our own Mass. He dipped the incense and smiled a half-smile as he saw the concentration on our faces.

"*Sh'ma yisrael,*" he whispered, "*adonai elohenu, adonai echad!*"

Kev closed the thurible and grinned. Father turned back to the altar and we knelt as he incensed the host and the chalice.

Watching Father O'Phelan, I suddenly realized what he had done for us.

I pictured a dim room with a long table. A young man stood at its head surrounded by his friends....

As Monsignor bent over the eucharistic bread I thought of an apostle named John, after whom I was named.

"Why is this night different from all other nights?" the youngest apostle asked Jesus at that first Mass.

"Because, my son," the resonant voice in my mind responded, "on this night God delivered his people from bondage."

The Flight of the Arrow

To say that Father O'Phelan was all things to all men would be an overstatement. But to say that he had a way of being pretty much what was needed as the situation required, might be fairly close to the truth.

Father was curious to the point of being comical. Whenever a new experience presented itself Father would become obsessed with it until he had learned all he could about whatever it was. He knew so many people that it was rightly said he could call on someone for any occasion or any need.

By the same token, Father was unstinting in his devotion to his parishioners. Many times I had seen him arrive back at St. Columbkille after a long night at the hospital only to be told that another parishioner had need of him.

"Ah, well," he would sigh, taking a scone or two from the kitchen sideboard instead of his plate of supper, which Mrs. Hanrahan had put in the oven to keep warm. And off he would go.

Nothing, however, prepared us for what we witnessed during the illness and passing of Regis O'Neill, Brian's younger brother. When

Regis was almost twelve, he was stricken with a strange illness that seemed to sap the very strength from his active, young body.

"Like a cancer in his blood," Brian told us sadly. He said his mother had told him to ask all his friends to pray for a miracle. It seemed that was all that could possibly save his younger brother.

Because of Regis's illness, Father O'Phelan became a regular visitor at the O'Neill apartment. Often he would stop Brian or one of us to ask after the young boy and his face reflected his genuine concern for Regis when we told him what we knew.

"Ah," was all he could say. "Perhaps tomorrow will bring us some better news."

One sunny afternoon several of us were sitting around the stoop of the O'Neill apartment when Father came on by on his way to visit Regis. It was a quiet afternoon and, since we were as important as anyone else at the moment, Father sat on the worn stoop along with us and asked what Regis might be interested in that would bring up his spirits.

"He's crazy about the last movie he saw," Brian laughed. "It was *The Adventures of Robin Hood* and he's been talking about it non-stop, Father! He really liked it!"

"Robin Hood!" Father O'Phelan was instantly alert. "I've loved that tale since I was a boy! I think I've still got my book!"

The next afternoon Father hurried back to the O'Neill flat with a worn book in his hand. It was Howard Pyle's classic tale, *The Adventures of Robin Hood and His Merrie Men of Sherwood.*

For the next few weeks Father spent a part of each afternoon with young Regis O'Neill. Oftentimes some of us would be there, too, listening as Father regaled us all with his uncanny knowledge of the mythical brigand.

"He wasn't really called Robin Hood, you know," Father told us excitedly, "He was the Earl of Locksley but his companions called him 'Robyn of the Hood.'"

He wrote down the name so we could commit it to memory. Regis, weak from the medicine and from his illness, beamed up from a mountain of pillows.

Mrs. O'Neill, a very large woman with a florid face and an instinct for mothering everyone who crossed her path, occasionally stood at the door to the boys' room, which had become Regis's world.

"I should think ye might be praying with our Regis," she gently chided Father one afternoon as we came out into the tiny living room.

"I am, Mrs. O'Neill."

Father's look penetrated the grieving mother and we saw a glimmer of understanding light up her eyes.

"Thank you, Father!" Mrs. O'Neill muttered as tears welled up.

Father spun tales about Robin and Little John, about Much, the Miller's son, and Maid Marian who languished in the castle until her rescue could be accomplished by Robin himself. He told about the famous competition at Nottingham where Robin's arrow split that of the best archer in all of England, and how the steely-eyed Sheriff of Nottingham tried to connive and cajole Robin's fellow thieves into giving him over for the hangman.

"But he was a thief, Father!" Brian once protested.

"And so was Dismas, the thief who was crucified alongside Jesus. His greatest 'theft' was the stealing of heaven itself, simply by asking Jesus to remember him!"

We laughed. Father was right. The way he said it could only be taken one way.

"Did Robin Hood go to heaven, Father?" Ritchie Saperstein asked innocently. Like the rest of us, Ritchie had listened for so long to Father O'Phelan that Robin Hood had become a real person rather than a mythical legend.

Father's eyes glazed over a bit as he looked out the window. His hand rested on Regis's warm brow and he caressed the boy's hair. We could tell from the way he spoke that the story was continuing.

"When it came time for Robyn of the Hood—who had been called the Prince of Thieves—to prepare for his death, he bade John Little, his trusted friend, to take his bow and hold it while he knocked an arrow on his string."

Holding his hands stretched out like one holding a longbow, the priest passed the imaginary weapon to the boy who lay almost motionless in the bed. Regis O'Neill reached up with his thin arms and took the unseen bow.

"When the arrow was knocked secure, John Little held his friend in his arms, supporting Robyn as he aimed his gray gooseshaft through the window of his hut."

Father put his arm around Regis's shoulder and let the boy lean on him. Regis was staring at the window with a fierce concentration which was evident to us all. He was totally immersed in the story.

Ritchie Saperstein and Bloke, sitting at the foot of the bed, leaned out of the way so that Regis's arrow might be true.

Slowly Regis pulled back the string of his invisible bow.

"John Little was mightily surprised at the strength of Robyn's pull," Father whispered, "and, when Robyn loosed the string, John Little could feel its thrust and knew that its flight would be true!"

Regis loosed his arrow. He sank back and Father took the imaginary bow.

"'Where my arrow lands,' Robyn said to Little John, 'there shall my bones be lain. I bid you break my bow that none may use her for good or for ill!' And, saying this, Robyn smiled on his friend and died. A just and noble man."

Father leaned down and kissed Regis's forehead. Regis was obviously tired, so Father nodded to the rest of us, letting us know that it was time to let Regis sleep.

"S'long, Regis," I mumbled, as usual.

"See ya," Regis said to each of us as we passed by on our way out of the room.

Denis Tracy winked at Regis and was gratified to see that Regis winked back.

Father O'Phelan was the last one to leave. We watched in the doorway as he stood up and made the Sign of the Cross over Regis, as he always did.

"Hey Father!" Regis grinned with a newfound strength. "Give me my bow back!"

Father laughed and handed Regis the imaginary bow. The boy took it and caressed the length of the smooth, invisible wood.

We left the apartment and went out into the warm afternoon.

Regis O'Neill died during the night. His parents were with him and so were his brothers and sisters. It was a peaceful end, Brian told us as he choked back his tears the next day. He said Regis was smiling and lucid until the very end.

"Then he just went on his way," Brian said.

Regis O'Neill's funeral was held in St. Columbkille. Monsignor Hanratty was the celebrant, and he wore white vestments for the Mass of the Angels since Regis was still only a boy. Fathers O'Phelan, O'Toole, and Smith wore their cassocks and surplices as they sat in the sanctuary. The boys' choir, in which Regis had sung, chanted flawlessly throughout the service for their friend. The entire church was filled to overflowing.

After the Mass, we processed to the gravesite in the little parish cemetery behind the church. There Monsignor said the final prayers. Then, handing the incense pot back to my brother, Kevin, Monsignor looked over at Father O'Phelan and smiled a little as he stepped back out of the way. Father, also smiling, though a bit sadly, stepped out of the crowd of mourners and stood by the plain little coffin poised over the open grave.

In his hands he held a bow and arrow.

Father stood for a long while just looking at Regis's coffin. Then, he looked over at Brian and motioned for him to come by his side.

He handed Brian the arrow, then slowly, the priest lifted the bow and bent his knee at the same time.

In a flash, Father brought the bow down on his knee.

The wood cracked like a rifle shot in the silence of the moment, and the bow was split in two pieces, joined only by the string.

Father placed the broken bow on top of the coffin. Brian handed Father the arrow and the priest put it with the broken bow.

Not a single word had been said.

After the funeral Father gathered Regis's friends together and took us all over to the park to stand by the lagoon. Even though it was plain daylight and a warm day, a park guard had built a small campfire as Father had asked him to do.

We stood by watching as Father O'Phelan put several arrows point-first in the fire.

"And Robyn's friends gathered in Sherwood to shoot an arrow, blazing with fire, into the still lake so that each may be joined with their friend in God's kingdom."

Father O'Phelan was ending the tale we had been sharing since he learned of Regis's love for the story of Robin Hood.

"And each," he said, handing the bow first to Brian, "took his arrow and shot it in the air."

Brian shot his flaming arrow. It arched and fell into the still lagoon a dozen yards from the shore.

Each of us shot a blazing tribute—me, Bloke, my brothers Danny and Kevin, Denis Tracy, Ritchie and Noam Saperstein, and Regan O'Farrell.

When we had all shot our arrows, in utter silence and awesome solemnity, Father took the final arrow and knocked it on the bowstring.

"And the last arrow," he said, tears streaming down his cheeks, "was that of his good and faithful servant, John Little whom he had called 'Little John.'"

The arrow arched higher than had ours. The flame blazed strong and we could hear it shudder in the wind of its flight. Then it bent and plunged headlong into the lagoon, hissing as it went out.

We stood there, silent in our thoughts.

In retrospect, I imagine we might have been taken to task for honoring our friend in such a "pagan" way. I imagine Father O'Phelan might have had his critics for the way he led a young boy through the shadow of death into the brightness of God's own light.

But for me and for my friends, the gentle, unprepossessing and self-effacing priest—the servant of the servants of God—forever etched himself in our minds and hearts as John Little, humble friend and companion to Robyn of the Hood.

Robyn had given his friend the nickname "Little John" because he stood as tall as a giant. And to us, that's how Father O'Phelan always stood—and always will!

Of Related Interest...

A World of Stories for Preachers and Teachers*
*and all who love stories that move and challenge
William J. Bausch

These 350 tales aim to nudge, provoke, and stimulate the reader and listener, to resonate with the human condition, as did the stories of Jesus.

0-89622-919-X, 534 pp, $29.95 (B-92)

REVISED AND EXPANDED
BESTSELLER
Catholic Customs and Traditions
A Popular Guide
Greg Dues

From Candlemas, to the Easter candle, through relics, Mary, the saints, indulgences, the rosary, mystagogia, laying on of hands, and more, the author traces the vast riches of the traditions, customs, and rituals of Roman Catholics.

0-89622-515-1, 224 pp, $12.95 (C-14)

600 Blessings and Prayers from Around the World
Compiled by Geoffrey Duncan

The blessings here cover an amazing array of occasions and needs; they are exuberant as well as practical, poetic and prayerful, simple and profound.

1-58595-134-X, 400 pp, $19.95 (J-90)

Blessed Are You
A Prayerbook for Catholics
Gwen Costello

The beautiful keepsake book contains daily prayers, prayers for feasts, seasons, and special occasions, and traditional prayers. Ideal for personal use as well as a great gift book.

1-58595-260-5, $19.95

TWENTY-THIRD PUBLICATIONS

185 WILLOW STREET • PO BOX 180 • MYSTIC, CT 06355
TEL: 1-800-321-0411 • FAX: 1-800-572-0788
Bayard E-MAIL: ttpubs@aol.com • www.twentythirdpublications.com